# THE ILLUSTRATED DIRECTORY OF
# WATCHES

## JAMES WILSON

**CHARTWELL
BOOKS, INC.**

This edition published in 2012 by CHARTWELL BOOKS, INC.
A division of BOOK SALES, INC.
276 Fifth Avenue Suite 206
New York, New York 10001
USA

ISBN-13  978-0-7858-2914-0

Printed in Indonesia

# Contents

# A. Lange & Sohne

A. Lange was founded in Glashutte, Germany in 1845. Glashutte was located in the Saxon region of Germany (a few miles south of Dresden), an area noted for its inventors and technicians. The nineteenth-century Saxon Elector, Frederick Augustus 1 actively promoted scientific advances in his kingdom, and was especially interested in clocks and watches. Ferdinand Adolph Lange began his watch making career as an apprentice to a master clockmaker. He then founded the Glashutte pocket watch factory, with an ambition to create high quality timepieces. When Ferdinand Lange died in 1875 (at the early age of sixty), the company was continued by his sons Emil and Richard, and later his grandson. A. Lange & Sohne remained in continuous production until 1945, when the factory was bombed on the final day of World War Two. Glashutte became marooned in the communist area of East Germany, and A. Lange & Sohne production lapsed for over forty years. After the re-unification of Germany, Frederick Lange's great-grandson Walter Lange re-established the company in 1990, and presented his first collection of watches just four years later. This included the Lange 1 wristwatch with its patented outsize date and off-center dial configuration. The company continues to match high quality watches using traditional skills aligned with modern technology. Today, Walter Lange has four-hundred-and-seventy employees, and his company is based in Glashutte once more.

(above) A. Lange Tourbillon Perpetual Calendar in 18K pink gold. Calendar with outsize date, day of the week display, moon-phase display, day/night indicator, and leap year indicator.

*A. Lange & Sohne*

(left) A. Lange Lange 1 platinum gentleman's watch with off-center hour dial, 2000. Transparent case back, subsidiary seconds dial, and oversized date.

*Image courtesy of Antiquorum Auctioneers*

(above) A. Lange Lange 1 in pink gold, 2002. 18K pink gold, water-resistant, off-center hour dial, and oversized date.

*Image courtesy of Antiquorum Auctioneers*

(left) A. Lange Lange 1 Tourbillon, 2002. Limited edition watch in platinum with visible one-minute tourbillon regulator, off-center dial, and oversized date.

*Image courtesy of Antiquorum Auctioneers*

(left) A. Lange Platinum Cabaret, circa 2005. Rectangular platinum watch with large date, black dial made from solid silver.

*Image courtesy of Antiquorum Auctioneers*

(below) A. Lange Die Grosse Fliegeruhr matte nickeled pilot's wristwatch from the 1940s. Over-sized watch with indirect center seconds, black dial, and signed case and movement.

*Image courtesy of Antiquorum Auctioneers*

(left) A. Lange B-Uhr German military watch from the 1940s. Oversized, anti-magnetic, nickel-silver navigator's timepiece.

*Image courtesy of Antiquorum Auctioneers*

(below) A. Lange Saxonia Automatic 18K white gold, the case set with brilliant-cut diamonds. Self-winding with subsidiary seconds. Hand-stitch crocodile strap.

*A. Lange & Sohne*

# Accurist

Asher and Rebecca Loftus founded Accurist in 1946. They were located in the Clerkenwell district of London, England. They made their watches entirely from Swiss components, but ensured that they were competitively priced. The company famously promoted the twenty-one jewel lever movement in their timepieces. Accurist always made fashionable watches and these were favored by many prominent people including Princess Anne, The Beatles, and the British model Twiggy. The company became increasingly successful in the 1960s and opened their own factory in La Chaux de Fonds, Switzerland. In the 1970s,

Accurist switched to quartz movements, and in 1983, the founders' son Andrew Loftus moved production to Japan. By 1993 Accurist was the second largest watch producer in the United Kingdom. In 1995, Accurist became the only watch brand to have an association with the Royal Observatory at Greenwich, London. The Observatory is particularly significant to the watch-making industry as it is the home of Greenwich Mean Time. Accurist continues to be a successful family-owned company, with its headquarters in London.

(right) Accurist white ceramic watch with white enamel multi-dial.
*Accurist*

(left) Accurist 9K gold watch with manual wind and subsidiary center seconds. Two-piece case.
*littlecogs.com*

(right) Accurist gold tone ladies' watch set with Swarovski crystals. Mother or pearl dial. Current production.
*Accurist*

(right) Accurist rectangular black ceramic watch with black enamel dial. Shadow indexes and single diamond. Current model.
*Accurist*

(above) Accurist black and gold ion-plated watch with black dial. Currently available.
*Accurist*

(right) Accurist stainless steel ladies' watch with mother of pearl dial set with Swarovski crystals. Current model.
*Accurist*

# Audemars Piguet

Audemars Piguet was founded in 1875 by two partners with a passion for precision, Jules-Louis Audemars and Edward Auguste Piguet. The business is still owned and run by the original families and retains its original commitment to excellence. It is the oldest fine watchmaker never to have left the ownership of its founding families. The company was established in the town of Le Brassus, Switzerland and is still there today.

The history of Audemars Piguet is littered with technical milestones. In 1892, the partners introduced the first minute repeater wristwatch. In 1915, they launched the smallest five-minute repeater ever made, with a diameter of just 15.8 millimeters. The first jumping-hour wristwatch was launched in 1924, followed by the world's thinnest pocket watch in 1925, the first skeletonized pocket watch in 1934, and the world's thinnest wristwatch in 1946. The popularity of Audemars Piguet's ultra thin dress models was largely responsible for the company's resurgence in the post-Depression years.

Audemars Piguet's seminal Royal Oak model was introduced in 1972. It was the first steel high-end sports watch, and debuted at that year's watchmakers' fair at Basel, Switzerland. The watch was fitted with a distinctive octagonal bezel, secured with eight small, visible screws. It also had simple metal bar hour markers. Although the watch was expensive with a launch price of 3,300 Swiss francs, it was an instant success. 1994 saw the launch of the company's first wristwatch with Grande and Petite Sonnerie (a quarter repeater striking on two gongs). The Equation of Time model appeared in 2000, complete with the times of sunrise and sunset. Audemars Piguet's first wristwatch with a carbon case and movement debuted in 2008. This was a particularly striking-looking timepiece with its matt black case and visible carbon movement.

Even today, all Audemars Piguet watches are completely handmade, and several iconic models, including the Royal Oak remain in production. Each of these watches takes around seven-hundred to a thousand hours of work to complete. A heavily diamond-encrusted Royal Oak Offshore watch currently retails for over a million dollars.

Audemars Piguet's ambassadors include many famous sportsmen and women, including the tennis player Novak Djokovic, and golfers Lee Westwood and Rory McIlroy. The company's partners include Russia's Bolshoi ballet and the Spanish Riding School in Vienna, Austria.

(left) Audemars Piguet tantalum and pink gold perpetual calendar watch, circa 1996. Astronomic, skeletonized, self-winding, and water-resistant.
*Image courtesy of Antiquorum Auctioneers*

(left) Audemars Piguet white gold Lady's emerald and diamond quartz Royal Oak, circa 1990s. Octagonal, 18K white gold, set with baguette emeralds and diamonds.
*Image courtesy of Antiquorum Auctioneers*

(right) Audemars Piguet Royal Oak. Stainless steel watch with screw-down hexagonal crown.
*Image courtesy of Antiquorum Auctioneers*

(above) Audemars Piguet stainless steel Royal Oak Automatic, 2001. Octagonal with center seconds, self-winding, water-resistant.
*Image courtesy of Antiquorum Auctioneers*

(right) Audemars Piguet Grand Sonnerie Carillon, Genève, 2002. Limited edition platinum watch with Grande et Petite Sonnerie.

*Image courtesy of Antiquorum Auctioneers*

(below) Audemars Piguet Royal oak Offshore Automatic, circa 2007. Octagonal, self-winding watch in 18K white gold and orange rubber, with diamond-set bezel.

*Image courtesy of Antiquorum Auctioneers*

(above) Audemars Piguet Royal Oak Offshore. Dial decorated with Mega Tapisserie pattern, gold applied hour-markers. Rubber bracelet.

*Audemars Piguet , le Brassus*

(right) Audemars Piguet 18K white gold Equation du Temps St. Tropez, 2010. Astronomic with perpetual calendar, sunrise and sunset set for the French city of St. Tropez.

*Image courtesy of Antiquorum Auctioneers*

(below and below right) Audemars Piguet Twenty Dollar Coin, 1975. 18K yellow gold with gold coin from 1904. Hinged inner case, straight lugs.

*Image courtesy of Antiquorum Auctioneers*

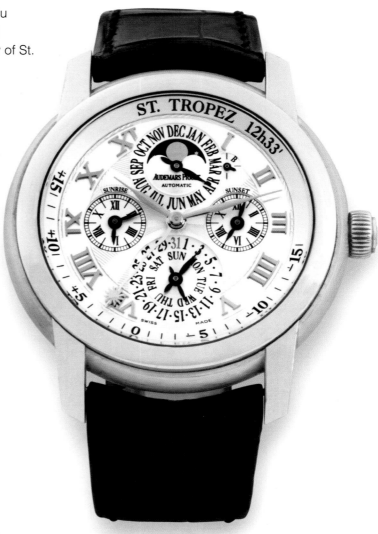

(below) Audemars Piguet 18K yellow gold quartz watch set with diamonds and rubies, 1990s. Oval, water-resistant.

*Image courtesy of Antiquorum Auctioneers*

(above and right) Audemars Piguet Backwinder in 18K white gold and diamonds, 1940s.

*Image courtesy of Antiquorum Auctioneers*

# *Avia*

The Avia watch-making company was registered in Switzerland in 1910. From the beginning, the company prided itself on producing innovative wristwatches, and pioneered the development of quartz watches in the 1970s. Their current philosophy is to produced high-quality and attractive watches at very affordable prices. Avia was bought by the Fossil fashion group in 2001. Fossil are one of the leaders in fashion watch design.

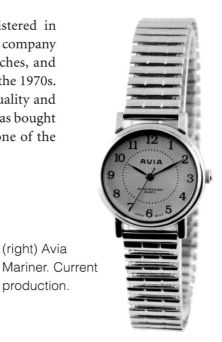

(right) Avia Mariner. Current production.

(left) Avia ladies'. Stainless steel, expandable bracelet. Current model.

(below left) Avia 1910. Gold-plated, silver dial. Current model.

(below right) Avia high-shine stainless steel. Silver dial, current model.

(above) Avia manual wind 9K gold watch with two-piece case. Center seconds, Hallmarked London, England 1973.

littlecogs.com

(above) Avia stainless steel case. Current production.

# Baume & Mercier

Baume & Mercier was founded in 1918 by William Baume and Paul Mercier, but the company's origins are almost a century older. The Baume family set up their watch shop in Switzerland's Jura region in 1830, and they were soon manufacturing their own timepieces. These watches were awarded many prestigious prizes around the world. Baume's business partner, Paul Mercier, was born in Odessa, Russia, and was an astute business man. He took charge of the commercial side of the business, while William Baume supervised the manufacture of their watches.

The company's excellent reputation helped them to survive the Depression, but both original partners left the business in 1937. Baume & Mercier was taken over by the famous jeweler Constantin de Gorski and his partner Robert Peron. The company flourished, and launched one of their most iconic models, the Marquise. This was a lady's "jewelry watch" where the timepiece was set into a jeweled bangle. In 1952, Baume & Mercier moved its production facilities to the famous watch-making village of Le Brassus in Switzerland's Jura Valley. In the 1960s, the brand repositioned itself as an affordable luxury brand, and has continued to inhabit this market niche. In 1972, Baume & Mercier launched the Mimosa and Galaxie ladies' models, followed by the Riviera and Stardust watches in 1973. The Riviera is a twelve-sided stainless steel sport watch, while the Stardust has an onyx dial encircled by a halo of small diamonds. The Linea collection followed in the 1980s.

In 1988, Baume & Mercier was bought by the Richemont Group, the parent company of many luxury brands including Piaget, Cartier, Jaeger-le-Coultre, Van Cleef & Arpels, Dunhill, and Montblanc. Financial stability led to a creative flowering, and several new lines were launched including the Hampton (1994), the Catwalk (1997), and the Capeland. More new ranges followed including the Classima, Diamant, and Haute Horologie William Baume. Many of the post-Richemont ranges are still in production today.

The company now produces its watches in Les Brenets in the Swiss Jura. Its headquarters remain in Geneva, Switzerland.

Baume & Mercier's company motto is "Life is about moments." The company has appointed several famous ambassadors for its products, including Gwyneth Paltrow in 2011.

(left) Baume & Mercier yellow gold chronometer, 1940s.
*Courtesy of Antiquorum Auctioneers*

(below) Baume & Mercier, Genève Riviera, 18K yellow gold quartz with center seconds.
*Courtesy of Antiquorum Auctioneers*

(above) Baume & Mercier Capeland, 2012. Automatic steel chronograph.
*Baume & Mercier*

(above) Baume & Mercier steel and diamond Linea, current model. Quartz movement with date and chronograph.
*Baume & Mercier*

(right) Baume & Mercier red gold Classima, current model. Automatic and date.
*Baume & Mercier*

(above) Baume & Mercier 14K yellow gold lady's dress watch, 1960s.

*Trebor's Vintage Watches*

(right) Baume & Mercier Formula S, 2000s. Stainless steel, quartz powered asymmetric chronograph.

*Courtesy of Antiquorum Auctioneers*

(below) Baume & Mercier manual wind 18K yellow gold lady's watch, 1970s. Dark blue dial, fully signed.

*Trebor's Vintage Watches*

(left) Baume & Mercier Capeland automatic chronograph, 2012. Self-winding, water-resistant, stainless steel watch with red telemeter.

*Courtesy of Antiquorum Auctioneers*

(below) Baume & Mercier yellow gold Hampton City automatic, 2004. Rectangular watch with date.

*Courtesy of Antiquorum Auctioneers*

(left) Baume & Mercier 14K yellow gold quartz lady's model. Integrated gold mesh bracelet.

*Trebor's Vintage Watches*

(left) Baume & Mercier Traction Avant, 1960s. Watch modeled on Citroen car. 18K pink and white gold, diamond headlights, ruby rear light.
*Courtesy of Antiquorum Auctioneers*

(right) Baume & Mercier 18K white gold oval lady's watch, 1980s.
*Courtesy of Antiquorum Auctioneers*

(below) Baume & Mercier rectangular quartz Hampton, current model. Steel with curved sapphire crystal. Alligator strap.
*Baume & Mercier*

(below) Baume & Mercier solid 14K yellow gold square-shaped lady's dress watch, 1970s. Leather strap. Signed case and movement.
*Trebor's Vintage Watches*

# *Benrus*

Benrus was founded by Benjamin Lazrus in 1921. Lazrus was from a Jewish-Romanian background. He located his first shop at 206, Broadway, New York City. His brothers Oscar (an attorney) and Ralph (a salesman) also worked in the business. Each brother took a turn at being president of the company. In 1923, Lazrus trademarked the Benrus name. Originally, Lazrus mended watches before starting to sell imported timepieces. By 1930, Benrus had begun to retail its own products. Lazrus bought a factory in the watchmaking town of La Chaux-de-Fonds in Switzerland's Jura region, where he manufactured his own Swiss movements. These were then imported into the United States, and fitted into American-made cases. Despite the war, Lazrus continued to import his Swiss mechanisms, and supplied Benrus watches to United States servicemen. In the post-war years, Benrus launched their famously complicated calendar watch. This was followed by their "Embraceable" bangle watch, their "Citation" model, and their "Dial-o-Rama" watches. Their exaggerated looks reflected the Retro-Modern styling cues that were popular in the 1940s.

The company grew exponentially in the 1950s and became the third largest watchmaker in America. Benrus also became a major shareholder in America's largest watchmaker, the Hamilton Watch Company. This time not only saw the launch of Benrus's famous waterproof watches, but the company also began to offer two cheaper model ranges, the Belforte and Sovereign. The company also made Dick Tracey and Disney character watches. Benrus were always savvy about their advertising, and the 1960s saw Jerry Lewis appearing in their advertisements.

The Lazrus family sold the company to Victor Kiam in 1967. Kiam sold many Benrus watches to army and navy military personnel fighting in the Viet Nam war. He also launched the Destino line of fashion watches, and the divers' watch-style "Orbit" in 1974. But the company was finally beaten by the introduction of cheap electric watches that flooded the American market in the second half of the decade, and filed for bankruptcy in 1977.

(above) Benrus stainless steel manual wind watch, 1960s.

*Trebor's Vintage Watches*

(above) Benrus automatic with date, 1960s. Gold plated case.

*Trebor's Vintage Watches*

(left) Benrus digital read jump hour watch, 1950s. Retro-modern-styled watch in chrome and stainless steel.

*Trebor's Vintage Watches*

---

(right) Benrus Diamond Flower model, circa 1950. 18K white gold and diamond watch with concealed dial.

*Image courtesy of Antiquorum Auctioneers*

(below right) Benrus 1940s scalloped tank model with textured dial.

*Trebor's Vintage Watches*

---

(below) Benrus Wristalarm, 1960s. Manual wind front-opening watch with alarm.

*Trebor's Vintage Watches*

---

(left) Benrus Shockresist watch, 1950s. 14K pink gold, white gold hands.

*Image courtesy of Antiquorum Auctioneers*

# *Blancpain*

Blancpain claims to be the oldest watchmaker in the world. The company was founded in 1735 by Jehan-Jacques Blancpain, and located in his farmhouse home in Switzerland's Jura region. The Blancpain continued the company for many years, and Jehan-Jacques's great-grandson introduced the major innovation of the cylinder escapement. The company built their first factory in 1865 to increase their manufacturing volume and counter cheap American imports.

Blancpain launched the first automatic wristwatch in 1926. In 1932 the Blancpain family left the company, which was bought out by two members of staff. Despite this management change, the Blancpain company ethos remained unchanged. Blancpain introduced their frogman watches in the 1950s, including their iconic "Fifty Fathoms" model of 1953, as worn by Jacques Cousteau. The company struggled to survive in the 1970s, with competition from cheap American quartz watches and the worldwide recession of 1973. The management sold out to Jacques Piguet of the famous watchmaking family, and Jean-Claude Biver, a Blancpain employee. Under the new ownership, Blancpain carved out a market niche for expensive, handmade watches with many "complications." (Any indication beyond hours, minutes, and seconds is a complication.)

Today Blancpain make less than ten thousand watches a year, and concentrate on making traditional mechanical, round-case watches. Their current collection includes the Le Brassus, Villeret, L-Evolution, Fifty Fathoms, Tourbillon, GMT Alarm Watch, the Carrousel Minute Repeater, and the 1735 six-complication timepiece.

Blancpain has been a partner of the Lamborghini racing team since 2009.

(left) Blancpain Aqua Lung, hundred hours automatic watch with center seconds and date.

*littlecogs.com*

(right) Blancpain Villeret, 1990s. 18K yellow gold, stepped bezel.

*Courtesy of Antiquorum Auctioneers*

(above) Blancpain Aqua Lung, 1958. Stainless steel revolving black bezel.

*Courtesy of Antiquorum Auctioneers*

(right) Blancpain Fifty Fathoms, 2000s. Stainless steel, domed sapphire crystal.

*Courtesy of Antiquorum Auctioneers*

(above) Blancpain steel and gold watch with diamond bezel, 1990s. 18K yellow gold and stainless steel.

*Courtesy of Antiquorum Auctioneers*

(left) Blancpain 2100 Sport, circa 2000. Stainless steel watch with anti-reflective crystal.

*Courtesy of Antiquorum Auctioneers*

(above) Blancpain stainless steel Villeret with triple date and moon phases, 1990s.
*Courtesy of Antiquorum Auctioneers*

(right) Blancpain Day/Night, 2000. Self-winding, water-resistant, two time zone watch.
*Courtesy of Antiquorum Auctioneers*

(above) Blancpain triple date with moon phases, 1990s. 18K yellow gold and diamond watch.
*Courtesy of Antiquorum Auctioneers*

(right) Blancpain Air
Command, 1990s.
Stainless steel
chronograph with date.
*Courtesy of Antiquorum*
*Auctioneers*

(left) Blancpain
Rayville, 1970s. 18K
white gold and
diamond.
*Courtesy of Antiquorum*
*Auctioneers*

(right) Blancpain oval Concealed Time, 1970s.
18K white gold and diamond, gold textured
bracelet.
*Courtesy of Antiquorum Auctioneers*

(below) Blancpain platinum minute repeater,
2000.
*Courtesy of Antiquorum Auctioneers*

(right) Blancpain gold baguette,
circa 1960. 18K yellow gold with
tile-link bracelet.
*Courtesy of Antiquorum Auctioneers*

(below) Blancpain platinum skeleton Villeret, 1990s.

*Courtesy of Antiquorum Auctioneers*

(above) Blancpain Perpetual Calendar watch, 1990s. 18K yellow gold, self-winding watch with moon phases.

*Courtesy of Antiquorum Auctioneers*

(above) Blancpain L-Evolution manual wind watch, current model.
*Blancpain*

(right) Blancpain Tourbillon, 1990s. 18K yellow gold eight-day power reserve.
*Courtesy of Antiquorum Auctioneers*

(below) Blancpain women's flyback automatic chronograph with small seconds and date Black dial.
*Blancpain*

# Breitling

Breitling AG was founded by Leon Breitling in 1884. Leon was just twenty-four at the time. The fledgling company was based at St. Imier, Switzerland in the heart of the Jura watch-making region. From the beginning Breitling's market niche was in sturdy and technical timepieces for professionals and remains successful in this field. Gaston Breitling created the first wristwatch chronometer in 1915. The Chronomat remains Breitling's leading model, and the company is the world's only watch brand to equip all its models with chronograph-certified movements, which are ten times more accurate than ordinary quarts movements. Breitling manufactures its own movements which are then submitted to the Swiss Official Chronometer Testing Institute. Breitling began to make Navitimer watches for pilots during World War I, and still have a very close relationship with the aviation industry. The company sponsors the Reno Air Race, the Breitling Jet Team, and the Breitling Wingwalkers. In the years before World War II, Breitling became an official supplier to the Royal Air Force (in 1936).

Today, Breitling's three main manufacturing categories are watches for pilots, divers, and the luxury market. The company also makes aircraft instruments. As well as its close association with aviation, Breitling also makes watches for space travel. Astronaut Scott Carpenter wore a Cosmonaute Breitling into space.

The company confirmed this relationship with aviation in 1979 when pilot and watchmaker Ernest Schneider bought the company from the founder's grandson Willy Breitling.

The company ceased manufacturing in the early 1980s, beset by competition from cheap quartz watches. They re-started manufacture in 1982 and continued to introduce dynamic new models to the range. These included the Breitling Emergency. This watch had an integral radio transmitter that sends out a signal if the wearer is lost. The company also began a partnership with Bentley, and continues to make several Breitling Bentley and Flying B models.

Breitling is still owned by the Schneider family. The company headquarters is at Grenchen, Switzerland, and has over four-hundred employees. Their over-sized watches are now very popular, and have become accessories as well as practical instruments.

(left) Breitling Shark diver's automatic chronograph. Stainless steel case and bracelet.
*Trebor's Vintage Watches*

(right) Breitling Navitimer based on a model introduced in 1952 for professional pilots. This is the current version.
*Breitling AG*

(right) Breitling Superocean professional automatic, 2004. Stainless steel watch with gas escape valve.
*Courtesy of Antiquorum Auctioneers*

(above) Breitling Navitimer 18K yellow gold round button chronometer, 2000s.
*Courtesy of Antiquorum Auctioneers*

(right) Breitling Superocean self-winding chronometer with exceptional water resistance. Current model.
*Breitling AG*

(above) Breitling Datora Montbrillant in stainless steel, 2000.

*Courtesy of Antiquorum Auctioneers*

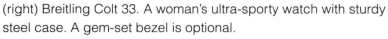

(above right) Breitling stainless steel Datora, 1960s. Round button chronograph, registers, triple date, and moon phases.

*Courtesy of Antiquorum Auctioneers*

(right) Breitling Colt 33. A woman's ultra-sporty watch with sturdy steel case. A gem-set bezel is optional.

*Breitling AG*

(left) Breitling Top Time, 2007. Cushion-shaped square button chronograph.
*Courtesy of Antiquorum Auctioneers*

(below) Breitling chronograph, 1940s. Two tone dial, gold-plated case.
*Trebor's Vintage Watches*

(above) Breitling travel chronograph with dual time zone system. Current model.
*Breitling AG*

(left) Breitling chronograph, 2010. Two time zone quartz watch.
*Courtesy of Antiquorum Auctioneers*

(above) Breitling Bentley
Motors T Speed, 2010. Thirty-
second chronograph.

*Courtesy of Antiquorum Auctioneers*

(above) Breitling Bentley Flying B
chronograph, 2010. Oversized curved
rectangular. 18K pink gold.

*Courtesy of Antiquorum Auctioneers*

(left) Breitling Montbrillant 47. Steel and rose
gold watch with black or silver dial. Current
production.

*Breitling AG*

(below) Breitling Televerket watch made for the Swedish government, 1960s. Antimagnetic stainless steel.

*Courtesy of Antiquorum Auctioneers*

(above) Breitling Yacht Timer, 1969. Stainless steel round button chronograph with revolving bezel.

*Courtesy of Antiquorum Auctioneers*

(right) Breitling Windrider Chronomat, circa 2010. 18K rose gold and steel.
*Courtesy of Antiquorum Auctioneers*

(above) Breitling yellow gold J Class diver's watch, 1990s.
*Courtesy of Antiquorum Auctioneers*

(left) Breitling Cockpit, 1990s. Limited edition watch made for the Japanese market.
*Courtesy of Antiquorum Auctioneers*

(above) Breitling Steel Sprint, 1968.
Antimagnetic stainless steel watch made to
celebrate the 1972 Munich Olympics.
*Courtesy of Antiquorum Auctioneers*

(right) Breitling Chronomat Evolution, 2008.
Stainless steel with red and silver dial.
*Courtesy of Antiquorum Auctioneers*

(above) Breitling Unitime Automatic, 1947.
Plated in rose gold.
*Courtesy of Antiquorum Auctioneers*

(left) Breitling Callisto 1884, from 1988.
Stainless steel round button chronograph.
*Courtesy of Antiquorum Auctioneers*

(above) Breitling Military watch made for Canada's NATO forces in the late 1960s. Stainless steel with screw back case.

*Trebor's Vintage Watches*

(left) Breitling Emergency Orbiter 3, 1999. Limited edition oversized 18K aviator's watch commemorating the Orbiter 3 balloon.

*Courtesy of Antiquorum Auctioneers*

# Bucherer

Bucherer was founded in 1888 by Carl-Fredrich Bucherer, when he opened his first watch and jewelry shop. Bucherer is still a family-run business, run by Carl-Fredrich's grandson Jorg B. Bucherer. Jorg took over the business in 1976. The company has always concentrated on retailing high-end timepieces and jewelry to wealthy customers, and now has thirty-three shops. Sixteen of these are in Switzerland's leading cities.

Carl-Fredrich's sons Carl Edouard and Ernst joined the business in 1915. Ernst became the official watchmaker to Kaiser Wilhelm II of Germany. In 1919, Ernst created the first genuine Bucherer timepieces in an Art Deco-style range of lady's watches. Shortly afterwards, the company opened a store in the famous Unter den Linden in Berlin, Germany. This combination of retailing and manufacture in a single company has often been compared to Tiffany. Bucherer are still very successful retailers and offer the largest selection of Rolex watches in the world. But the company has also introduced several iconic watches of their own to the discerning Swiss market. The iconic Archimedes Supercompressor diver's watch debuted in 1976 and the Patravi Chronograph GMT in 2001. The Alacria range appeared in 2003. Bucher strengthened the retail side of the business in 2004 when they expanded their sales operation to the United Sates.

Bucherer's current timepieces include the Novelties, Manero, Patravi, and Alacria ranges. The company specializes in highly decorated and technically intricate watches that are aimed at a wealthy clientele.

Bucherer has its headquarters in Lucerne, Switzerland and also has a company museum in the Swiss town of Lengnau. The company has around twelve hundred employees.

(left) Bucherer vintage watch, 1960s.
Automatic movement.

*Trebor's Vintage Watches*

---

(right) Bucherer Archimedes, 1997.
Limited edition of ninety-seven. 18K yellow and white gold, two-tone silver dial.

*Courtesy of Antiquorum Auctioneers*

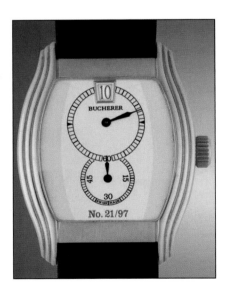

(right) Bucherer
Archimedes Automatic,
2000. Center seconds
and moon phases.
*Courtesy of Antiquorum Auctioneers*

(above) Bucherer Platinum Perpetual Calendar, 2000. Center
seconds, self-winding, water-resistant. 18K white gold.
*Courtesy of Antiquorum Auctioneers*

(right) Bucherer marquisate brooch watch, 1950. Silver swivel watch.
*Courtesy of Antiquorum Auctioneers*

(left) Bucherer Patravi GMT
chronograph, 2003. Stainless steel.
*Courtesy of Antiquorum Auctioneers*

(right) Bucherer rectangular 18K yellow
gold and diamond with articulated
bracelet, 1970s.
*Courtesy of Antiquorum Auctioneers*

(right) Bucherer Patravi Travel
Tec GMT chronograph, 2006.
*Courtesy of Antiquorum Auctioneers*

(right) Bucherer GMT Patravi
chronograph, circa 2000. Red
hand for second time zone.
*Courtesy of Antiquorum Auctioneers*

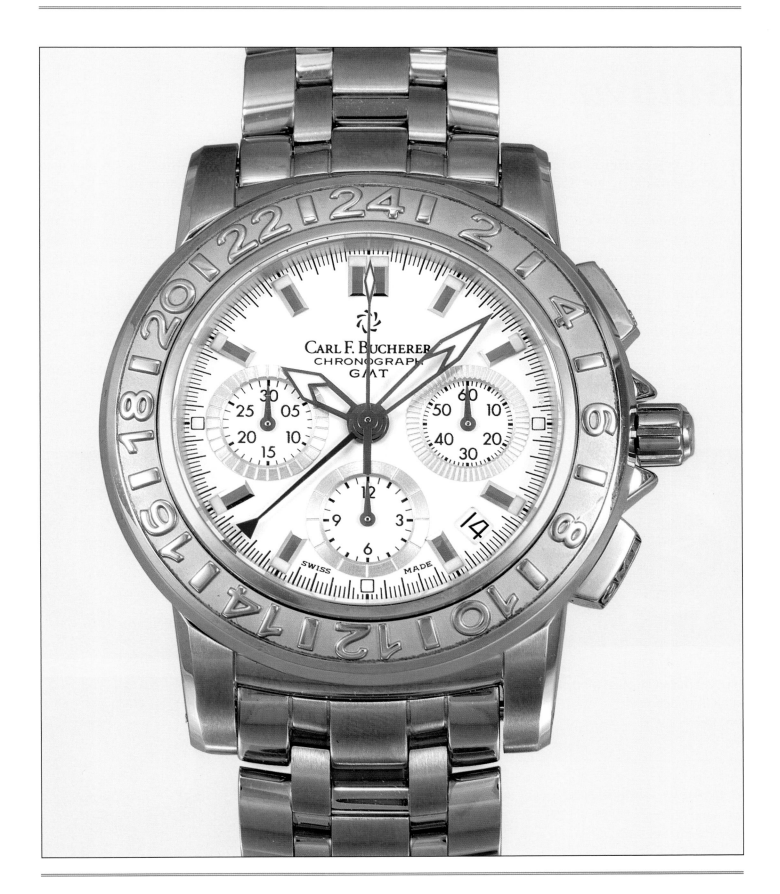

# Bulova

Joseph Bulova emigrated from Bohemia (modern Czechoslovakia) to the United States at the age of nineteen. He arrived in New York in 1870 and opened his first jewelry shop, J. Bulova in 1875. It was located at Maiden Lane in the famous jewelry district of Lower Manhattan. Bulova then decided to manufacture his own watches, and opened a factory in Bienne, Switzerland in 1912. It was at this factory that Bulova created the world's first assembly line dedicated to the construction of watches. He launched his first watch line in 1919. In 1930, Bulova constructed the Bulova Observatory in Midtown Manhattan. Always innovative, Bulova broadcast the first national radio commercial in 1926. The company later sponsored the first national television commercial. The company also used celebrities to endorse their products. Colonel Charles Lindbergh won the Bulova Watch Prize and also inspired the company's Lone Eagle watch. Over fifty-thousand examples of the model were sold. In 1928 Bulova invented the clock radio and manufactured the first electronic clock in 1931.

Bulova introduced their iconic Accutron model in 1960. It had an electric wind. Bulova Accutron timekeeping is now used aboard Air Force One. Bulova has also collaborated with NASA.

On October 4, 2000 New York City celebrated Bulova Day.

(above) Bulova manual wind chrome watch with subsidiary seconds.

*littlecogs.com*

(right) Bulova white gold-filled manual wind with diamond-cut markers, circa 1956.

*Trebor's Vintage Watches*

(right) Bulova Railway quartz 1979.

*Trebor's Vintage Watches*

# BULOVA

(below) Bulova military-style watch with black dial, 1962.
*Trebor's Vintage Watches*

(above) Bulova Deep Sea. Steel diver's watch, 1975.
*Courtesy of Antiquorum Auctioneers*

(right) Bulova Marine Star analogue chronograph. Stainless steel bracelet. Current production.
*Bulova*

47

(above) Bulova automatic yellow gold-filled, 1950.

*Trebor's Vintage Watches*

(right) Bulova Kirkwood chronograph with rubber strap. Current model.

*Bulova*

(below) Bulova 10K yellow gold case, 1940s.

*Courtesy of Antiquorum Auctioneers*

(below) Bulova manual wind, 1981. White and gold-colored metal.

*Trebor's Vintage Watches*

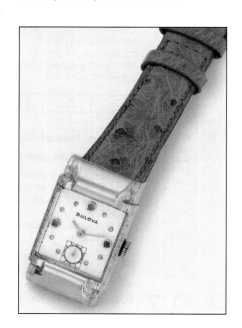

(below) Bulova Accutron 18K wristwatch and pocket watch.

*Courtesy of Antiquorum Auctioneers*

(above) Bulova Accutron, 1960s.
14K yellow gold electronic.
*Courtesy of Antiquorum Auctioneers*

(right) Bulova Accutron, circa
1974. Electronic stainless steel
watch.
*Courtesy of Antiquorum Auctioneers*

(above) Bulova Westfield
Watertite, 1941.
*Trebor's Vintage Watches*

(right) Bulova Accutron Railroad Approved. Stainless steel. Waterproof. Luminous hands. Vintage.

*littlecogs.com*

(below) Bulova Accutron, 1960s. 14K yellow gold, electronic.

*Courtesy of Antiquorum Auctioneers*

(left and above) Bulova
Accutron. Cushion-shaped,
skeleton. Gold-plated,
stainless steel back. Center
seconds. Vintage.

*littlecogs.com*

(above) Bulova Spaceview
skeletonized Accutron, 1968.

*Trebor's Vintage Watches*

(above) Bulova rectangular
chrome-nickel, 1930s.

*Courtesy of Antiquorum Auctioneers*

(above) Bulova Harley-
Davidson, stainless steel
analogue with luminous hands.
Current model.

*Bulova*

(right Bulova Harley-Davidson,
current production. Stainless
steel bracelet, black dial and
orange second hand.

*Bulova*

(below) Bulova Accutron Astronaut,
1960s. Cushion-shaped electronic
with center seconds.

*Courtesy of Antiquorum Auctioneers*

# Cartier

Louis-Francois Cartier took over the workshop of master jeweler Adolphe Picard in 1847. His shop was located in Paris, France. Cartier soon became famous for selling jewelry and luxury goods to wealthy Parisians and the royal families of Europe. His customers included the French Empress Eugenie and the English King Edward VII.

From the beginning, Cartier's ethos was luxury and innovation. Nowhere was this more apparent than in its wristwatches. The company created the first ladies' bracelet-watch in 1888, and in 1904 Cartier created a special wristwatch with a leather strap for his friend the Brazilian aviator Alberto Santos-Dumont. Santos-Dumont had been looking for a practical watch to wear when flying. Cartier's iconic Santos was the first flat watch with a square bezel. The Tonneau followed in 1906.

In 1907 the company made an agreement with watchmaker Edmond Jaeger to supply movements for their timepieces. Cartier also used movements from Piaget, LeCoultre, Movado, and Vacheron Constantin.

Cartier launched its first American store in 1909, located at 653 Fifth Avenue, New York City. This was also the year when Cartier patented their folding watchstrap buckle.

Cartier launched its iconic Tank watch in 1919. Many Tank variants followed including the Tank Louis Cartier, the Tank Chinoise, the Tank Divan, the Tank Americaine, and the Tank Francaise. The Cartier Baguette followed in 1926, the Tortue chronograph in 1928, the Mystery pocket watch in 1931, the Crash in 1967, and the Maxi Oval in 1968.

A group of investors bought the company in 1972, but Cartier's creative output was unstoppable. The gold and steel Santos de Cartier was launched in 1978, Les Musts de Cartier in 1981, the Pasha de Cartier in 1985, the Roadster in 2002, La Dona in 2006, the Ballon Bleu in 2008, and the Santos 100 Skeleton in 2009.

(above) Cartier Santos Galbee automatic. Stainless steel. 18K yellow gold bezel and decorative screws. Opaline dial.

(below) Cartier Santos automatic. Stainless steel. Roman numeral indicators.

(above) Cartier skeletonized flying tourbillon watch. 18K white gold and sapphire. 2012.

(below) Cartier Santos 100 automatic chronograph. 18K yellow gold. 2008.
*Courtesy of Antiquorum Auctioneers*

(above) Cartier Ellipse. 18K yellow gold, diamonds, and rose quartz. 2000.
*Courtesy of Antiquorum Auctioneers*

(left) Cartier Jumbo Baignoire Allongee. Jaeger-LeCoultre movement. 1969.\
*Courtesy of Antiquorum Auctioneers*

(right) Cartier Panther Décor. 18K white gold, diamonds, purple mother-of-pearl, and sapphire. 2012.

# Chopard

Louis-Ulysse Chopard founded his company in 1860 at the age of twenty-four. It was located in the village in Sonvilier in the Jura region of Switzerland. Despite fierce competition from many manufacturers, Chopard soon became well-known for its extreme craftsmanship. The company's motto was "Quality with the maximum possible work by hand." Chopard's son Paul Louis moved the company to Geneva in 1926. At this time, the company had a hundred-and-fifty members of staff. Chopard's grandson Paul Andre took over in 1943. As none of Paul Andre's sons wished to take over the Chopard business, he sold the company in 1963. The new owner was German watchmaker Karl Scheufele. His leadership injected creativity and innovation into the business. Several iconic Chopard watches were launched. The Happy Diamonds watch was introduced in 1976, followed by the St. Moritz in 1980, the Happy Sport in 1993, and the L.U.C. Tonneau in 2001. Karl's son and daughter Karl-Friedrich and Caroline are now the co-presidents of the company. Chopard is one of Switzerland's few luxury watchmakers that remain in family ownership, and the company celebrated its one-hundred-and-fiftieth anniversary in 2010. It is also famous for its lavish jewelry collection. The company is now the official partner of France's Cannes Film Festival.

(right) Chopard Happy Diamonds quartz watch, 1980s. 18K yellow gold and diamonds.
*Courtesy of Antiquorum Auctioneers*

(above) Chopard Mille Miglia stainless steel
chronograph, 2004.

*Courtesy of Antiquorum Auctioneers*

(right) Chopard steel and diamond Elton John, 2004.

*Courtesy of Antiquorum Auctioneers*

(left and inset)
Chopard Tourbillon
Heritage
chronometer
*Courtesy of Antiquorum*
*Auctioneers*

(right) Chopard white gold
dual time zone.
*Courtesy of Antiquorum*
*Auctioneers*

(below) Chopard Imperial
chronograph. 18K yellow
gold and diamonds.
*Courtesy of Antiquorum Auctioneers*

(left) Chopard Your Hour model. White gold and diamonds, 2000s.
*Courtesy of Antiquorum Auctioneers*

(below) Chopard Boutique, 2007. 18K white gold and diamonds.
*Courtesy of Antiquorum Auctioneers*

(below) Chopard Mille Miglia titanium chronometer, 2005.
*Courtesy of Antiquorum Auctioneers*

(above) Chopard Automatic, 1970s. 18K white gold and diamonds.
*Courtesy of Antiquorum Auctioneers*

(left) Chopard L.U.C. Chrono One.
A rare prototype from 2007.
*Courtesy of Antiquorum Auctioneers*

(right) Chopard Classique H
dual time, 2004
*Courtesy of Antiquorum Auctioneers*

# Chronographe Suisse

Chronographe Suisse watches were produced in the 1940s and 1950s. Mostly chronometer-style wristwatches, they were aimed at tourists to post-War Switzerland. Although some of the movements used in these timepieces were of poor quality, the cases were often gold-plated or solid gold and the watches themselves were very attractive. Surviving examples are quite valuable. The brand was re-launched latterly as Chronographe Suisse et Compagnie and concentrates on more luxurious and expensive timepieces.

(below and right) Chronographe Suisse. Four assorted watches from the 1940s and 1950s.

*Courtesy of Antiquorum Auctioneers*

(left) Chronographe Suisse antimagnetic chronograph. 18K pink gold, 1950s.
*Courtesy of Antiquorum Auctioneers*

(above) Chronographe Suisse 18K yellow gold chronograph, 1950s.
*Courtesy of Antiquorum Auctioneers*

(below) Chronographe Suisse 18K pink gold, 1940s.
*Trebor's Vintage Watches*

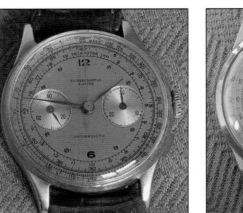

(right) Chronographe Suisse chronograph with register and subsidiary seconds. 18K pink gold, 1950s.
*Trebor's Vintage Watches*

# Chronographs

The word chronograph is made up from the Greek words for "time" and "writing," "chronos" and "graph." Early chronographs had tiny pens attached to them so the user could write on the dial. Frenchman Nicolas Mathieu Rieussec introduced the first true chronograph in 1821 and patented his invention in 1822. Rieussec's two-faced chronograph had been commissioned by the French King Louis XVIII who used it to time horse races.

A chronograph not only tells the time but can also be used for at least one other time measurement. These other functions track time independent of the time of day. Chronographs are also stopwatches and are usually equipped with at least one subsidiary dial. This means that even simple chronographs have complicated movements. More complex models have extremely intricate movements. Chronographs were one of the final mechanical watch complications to be invented and their complexity makes them larger and more expensive than ordinary watches. Chronographs were first used by sportsmen and soldiers, but were soon adopted by divers and race enthusiasts.

The first wrist-worn chronograph appeared around 1910. In 1968 Tag Heuer launched the first range of automatic chronographs, the Monaco, Autavia, and Carrera models. The Monaco was also the first square-cased chronograph. Chronograph watches soon became cutting-edge fashion accessories and many leading watch producers added them to their ranges.

Famous vintage chronographs include the 1957 Omega Speedmaster (which NASA used in its Apollo program), the Breitling Navitimer, the Zenith El Primero, and the Rolex Cosmograph (favored by Paul Newman). This popular complication has also inspired some interesting examples from less well-known manufacturers including Lanco, Gigandet, Officine Panerai, Jean-Mairet Gillman, and Dugena.

The complexity and versatility of the chronometer complication offers ambitious watchmakers a wonderful opportunity to demonstrate their technical skills and creativity.

(above) Heuer advertisement for the world's first automatic chronometer, the Carrera. Heuer launched this definitive model in 1968.

(above) Precimax three-button Swiss chronograph. Incabloc shock protection. Stainless steel.

*littlecogs.com*

(right) Allemann Swiss-made, single-button chronograph. Stainless steel, brushed silver dial.

*littlecogs.com*

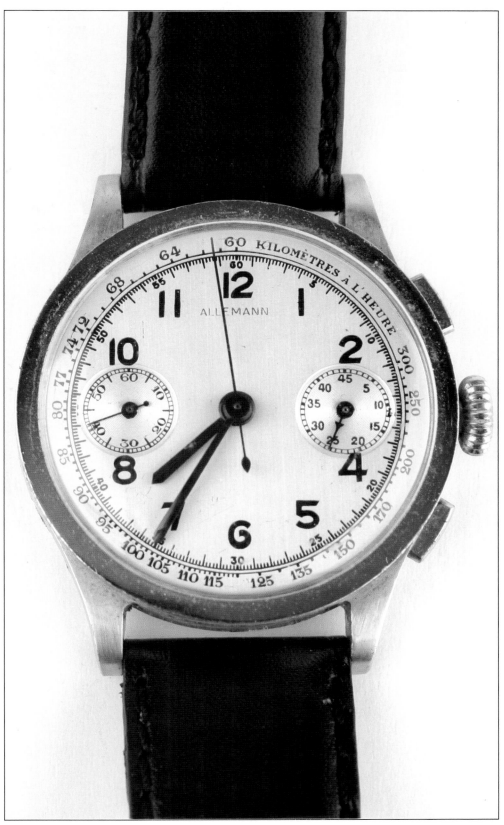

(left) Tag Heuer Monaco chronograph. Square, convex, square-button chronograph. 1990s
*Courtesy of Antiquorum Auctioneers*

(right) Franck Muller Swiss-made round-button chronograph. 18K pink gold. 1990s.
*Courtesy of Antiquorum Auctioneers*

(left) Gigandet Swiss three-button chronograph.
Incabloc shock protection.

*littlecogs.com*

(below) Jean-Mairet Gillman Alexandre III.
Swiss-made chronograph. 2000s.

*Courtesy of Antiquorum Auctioneers*

(above) Chaumet Class One. French-made, round-button
chronograph. Stainless steel and diamonds. 2000s.

*Courtesy of Antiquorum Auctioneers*

(left) Breuguet Transatlantique Type XX. 18K gold, Swiss-made, flyback chronograph. 2000s.

*Courtesy of Antiquorum Auctioneers*

(below) Graham Flyback automatic. Stainless steel, Swiss-made chronograph.

*Courtesy of Antiquorum Auctioneers*

(below) Wakmann three-resister chronograph. Stainless steel, Venus movement. Vintage.

*Trebor's Vintage Watches*

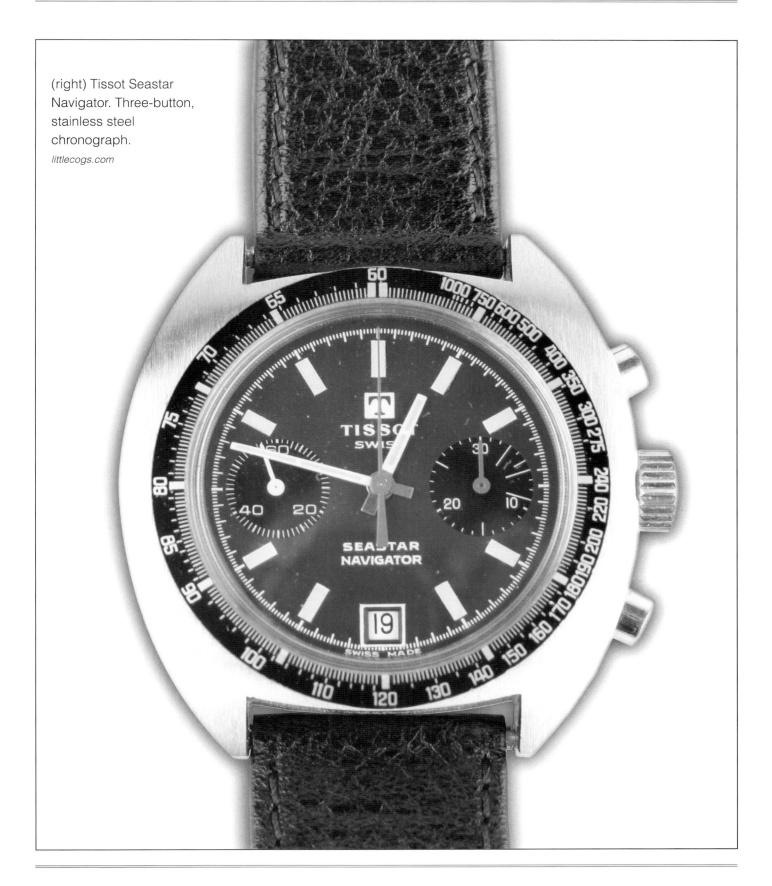

(right) Tissot Seastar
Navigator. Three-button,
stainless steel
chronograph.

*littlecogs.com*

(left) Dugena German-made chronograph. Three-dimensional baton indexes. Incabloc shock protection. Antimagnetic.

*littlecogs.com*

(above) Lorie triple-button chronograph. 1940s.

*Trebor's Vintage Watches*

(below) Fleuron Swiss-made chronograph. 18K pink gold, textured dial. 1950s.

*Trebor's Vintage Watches*

(above) Parmigiani Fleurier Kalpa. Swiss-made. Tonneau-shaped, oval-button chronometer. 18K pink gold. 2007.

*Courtesy of Antiquorum Auctioneers*

(left) Harry Winston Premier. American-made chronometer. 18K white gold. 1990s.
*Courtesy of Antiquorum Auctioneers*

(right) Daniel Roth automatic. 18K pink gold, double ellipse-shaped. Swiss-made chronometer. Late 1990s.
*Courtesy of Antiquorum Auctioneers*

(below) Cauny Prima Swiss-made, three-button chronograph. Superwaterproof. Antimagnetic. Raised baton indexes.
*littlecogs.com*

(right) Lanco Swiss-made three-button chronograph. Stainless steel. Antimagnetic, water-resistant. Incabloc shock protection.

*littlecogs.com*

(below) Longines Automatic. Tonneau-shaped, stainless steel case. Ivory dial.

*littlecogs.com*

(above) Consul Swiss chronograph. Stainless steel. Oval dial. Concealed lugs.

*littlecogs.com*

(left) Unsigned Swiss-made, three-button chronometer. Stainless steel. Rotating black and yellow bezel.

*littlecogs.com*

(left) Officine Panerai Luminor. Italian-made, automatic, square-button chronograph. Cushion-shaped, stainless steel. 2006.

*Courtesy of Antiquorum Auctioneers*

Le Jour Swiss three-button chronograph. Black dial, rotating bezel.

*littlecogs.com*

(above) Jean-Mairet Gillman World Time. Stainless steel, SMG black rubber strap. Swiss-made chronograph. 2009.

*Courtesy of Antiquorum Auctioneers*

(right) Ikepod Isopode Swiss-made, 18K pink gold chronograph. Flying-saucer-shaped. 2000s.

*Courtesy of Antiquorum Auctioneers*

(above) Hublot Big Ben Congo. Swiss-made, ceramic, skeleton chronograph. 2011.
*Courtesy of Antiquorum Auctioneers*

(left) Franc Vila Grand Sport Perpetual Calendar Swiss-made chronograph.
Large, deep, curved oval. 2000s.
*Courtesy of Antiquorum Auctioneers*

(left) Favre-Leuba. Swiss-made three-button chronograph.

*littlecogs.com*

(below) Avia Swiss-made, three-button chronograph. Blue dial, raised baton indexes. Incabloc shock protection, waterproof.

*littlecogs.com*

(right) Breitling Navitimer. Large, three-button chronograph. Stainless steel. Rotating, notched bezel.

*littlecogs.com*

(left) Bichrono
Hommage Only One
by delaCour,
Geneva. White gold,
red wood dial. Two
movements. 2004.
*Courtesy of Antiquorum*
*Auctioneers*

(above) Dugena three-button chronograph. Rotating black bezel. Raised baton indexes.

*littlecogs.com*

(right) Excelsior Park Decimal. Swiss-made, three-button chronograph. Stainless steel, silver dial.

*littlecogs.com*

(left) Seiko Automatic. Three-button chronograph. Stainless steel integral bracelet. Baton indexes. Luminous hands.

*littlecogs.com*

(right) Numa Swiss-made three-button chronograph. Stainless steel. Oval dial.

*littlecogs.com*

(right) Zenith El Primero ChronoMaster. Automatic, stainless steel, square-button chronograph. 2003.
*Courtesy of Antiquorum Auctioneers*

(left) Abercrombie & Fitch. Swiss-made chronometer. Staybrite stainless steel. 1947.
*Courtesy of Antiquorum Auctioneers*

(right) Franck Muller Perpetual Calendar Retrograde. Swiss-made, oval-button chronograph. Curved, tonneau-shaped. 18K white gold. 2001.
*Courtesy of Antiquorum Auctioneers*

(left) Tissot Seastar Navigator. Three-button, Swiss-made chronograph. Stainless steel, black bezel, luminous indexes.
*littlecogs.com*

(right) Bichrono Double Time
Zone by deLaCour, Geneva.
Oversized, curved,
tonneau-shaped. PVD-coated
steel. 2003.

*Courtesy of Antiquorum Auctioneers*

(left) Ferrari chronograph by Officine Panerai. Automatic. Cushion-shaped. 2007.

*Courtesy of Antiquorum Auctioneers*

(below) Zenith El Primero Port Royal. Square-button chronograph. PVD-coated titanium. 2007.

*Courtesy of Antiquorum Auctioneers*

(left) Heuer Carrera. First automatic chronograph. Stainless steel, blue dial, white sub-dials. 1968 or 1969.

*Trebor's Vintage Watches*

(below) Cvstos Challenge. Swiss-made, round-button chronograph. Tonneau-shaped. 2008.

*Courtesy of Antiquorum Auctioneers*

(above) TB Buti Italian-made flyback chronograph. Two time zones. Tonneau-shaped. Blue titanium and diamonds. 2009.

*Courtesy of Antiquorum Auctioneers*

(right) Belson Swiss-made two-register chronograph. 18K yellow gold. 1950s.

*Trebor's Vintage Watches*

(above) Hublot Super B. Swiss-made chronograph. 18K pink gold and Kevlar. 2006.

*Courtesy of Antiquorum Auctioneers*

(right) Tudor Chronotime automatic Oysterdate. 1985.

*Courtesy of Antiquorum Auctioneers*

# Citizen

Citizen was founded as the Shokosha Watch Research Institute in Tokyo, Japan in 1918. The company first used Citizen as a model name in 1924. Citizen was adopted as the company name in 1930. The company manufactured its first wristwatch in 1931 and is now one of the largest watch producers in the world. Citizen has always been a technologically advanced watchmaker. It launched Japan's first calendar watch in 1952. Citizen now offers a comprehensive range of dress, sport, and dive watches. Its Eco-Drive models are powered by a solar panel hidden under the watch face. Citizen has also made the world's slimmest LCD watch, the world's first voice recognition watch, and the Skyhawk A-T atomic flight chronograph.

Citizen's ambassadors include several famous sports personalities, including Paula Creamer and Matt Kenseth.

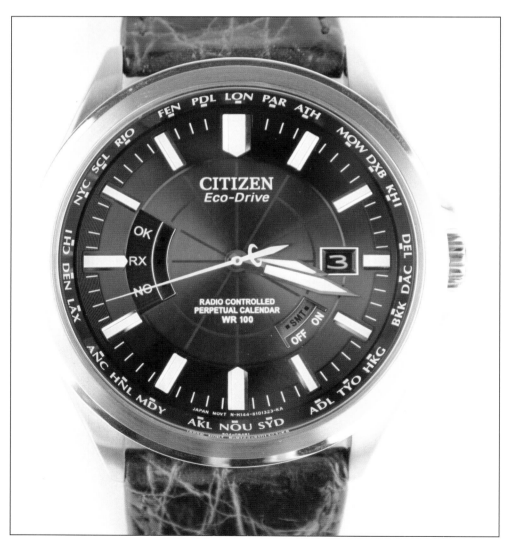

(left) Citizen Eco-Drive. Radio controlled chronograph. Perpetual calendar. World time. Current.

*littlecogs.com*

(below) Citizen Intellectus et Fortitudo quartz minute repeater. Stainless steel and yellow gold. 1992.

*Courtesy of Antiquorum Auctioneers*

(right) Citizen Eco-Drive. Steel case. Baton indexes. 2000s.

*Courtesy of Antiquorum Auctioneers*

(below) Citizen Red Arrow World Time. Stainless steel, three-button chronograph. Current.

*littlecogs.com*

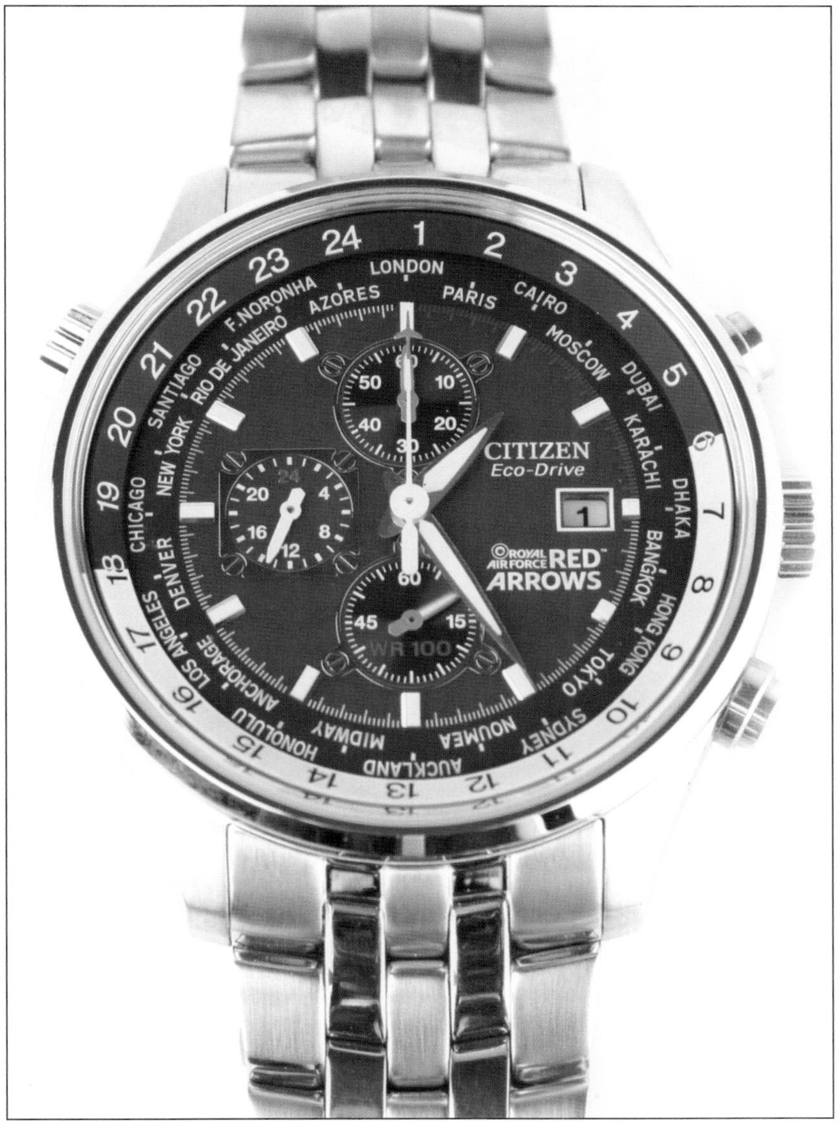

(above) Citizen Eco-Drive Octavia.
Octagonal. Stainless steel and diamonds.
Date. Current.

*littlecogs.com*

(right) Citizen Ultra-Thin Eco-Drive. Gold-
plated. Center seconds. Current.

*littlecogs.com*

(right) Citizen Eco-Drive WR200. Three-button chronograph.
Oversized, stainless steel. Current.

*littlecogs.com*

(left) Citizen Signature Eco-Drive. Three-dial chronometer. Stainless steel, black bezel. Current.

*littlecogs.com*

(below) Citizen Chronograph WR100M Eco-Drive. Stainless steel, black bezel. Current.

*littlecogs.com*

(above) Citizen Eco-Drive Perpetual Calendar WR300. Oversized, stainless steel. Rotating bezel. Date, center seconds. Current.

*littlecogs.com*

(right) Citizen
Signature Eco-Drive
Perpetual Calendar.
Midnight blue dial
and bezel. Luminous
hands. Current.

*littlecogs.com*

(below) Citizen Stiletto. Tonneau-shaped. Black PVD-coated, ultra-slim. Current.

*littlecogs.com*

(above) Citizen Eco-Drive. Diamond-set gold-colored steel. Mother-of-pearl dial. 2000s.

*Courtesy of Antiquorum Auctioneers*

(below) Citizen Eco-Drive.
Rectangular, stainless steel case and
strap. 2000s.
*Courtesy of Antiquorum Auctioneers*

(left) Citizen Eco-Drive. Diamond-set
steel and gold-colored steel. 2000s.
*Courtesy of Antiquorum Auctioneers*

(above) Citizen Eco-Drive.
Diamond-set steel case.
Mother-of-pearl dial. 2000s.
*Courtesy of Antiquorum Auctioneers*

# Concord

Concord was founded in Biel, Switzerland in 1908. The company's main business was producing books for the American market. Concord launched its iconic Private Label range of luxury watches in 1915, all constructed from precious metals and gemstones. In 1946 Concord launched another famous line of watches made from rare coins.

The company has continued to create new models. The Delirium I was launched in 1979, the Mariner in 1980, the Saratoga in 1986, the Sirius in 1991, and the Papillon collection in 1994. The La Scala geometric was announced in 1997, the La Scala steel in 2000, and the Delirium XXV in 2004.

The brand was re-positioned in 2007 moving away from pure luxury to a high-end, edgy modern styling. Many of the company's new models were skeletonized. Concord's new look was epitomized in the CI Quantum Gravity watch, launched in 2009.

(left) Concord Delirium Mariner, 1980s. Extra-flat quartz watch, 18K yellow gold.
*Courtesy of Antiquorum Auctioneers*

(right) Concord tonneau-shaped chronograph. Stainless steel and carbon fiber, 2009.
*Courtesy of Antiquorum Auctioneers*

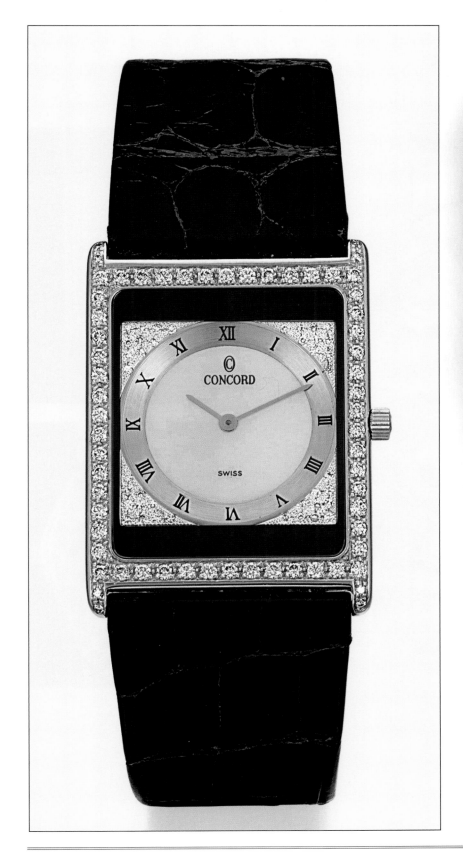

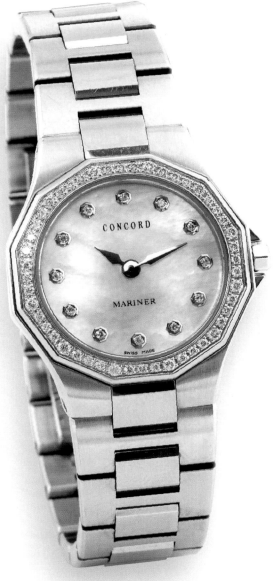

(above) Concord Mariner, 1990s.
Stainless steel and diamonds.
*Courtesy of Antiquorum Auctioneers*

(left) Concord Delirium Mariner,
1980s. Extra-flat watch in 18K white
gold and diamonds.
*Courtesy of Antiquorum Auctioneers*

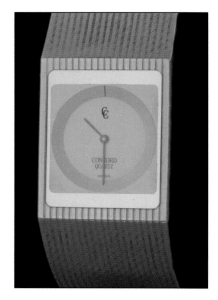

(below) Concord Quartz, 1990s. Extra-flat 18K yellow gold watch, baton hands.

*Courtesy of Antiquorum Auctioneers*

(above) Concord Astronomic, 1990s. 14K yellow gold.

*Courtesy of Antiquorum Auctioneers*

(above) Concord Triple Date, 2000s. 18K pink gold.

*Courtesy of Antiquorum Auctioneers*

# Corum

Corum is a relatively new Swizz watch making company. It was founded in 1955 by cousins Simone Ries and Rene Bannwarf. They joined Simone's father Gaston Ries at his workshop, and soon brought an avant garde creativity to his brilliant craftsmanship. Corum is located in La Chaux-de-Fonds at the center of the Swiss watch industry.

Corum's first important timepiece was the Twenty Dollar Liberty Eagle which was made from a real twenty dollar gold coin. Other notable watches soon followed. The Golden Tube watch of 1957, the Chinese Hat watch (1958), the Admiral's Cup sports watch (1960), the Rolls Royce watch (1976), the Bubble watch, and the World Series of Poker series all confirmed the company's reputation for originality. Corum's company ethos expresses this perfectly "boldness, distinction, and excellence." Corum is credited with introducing big watches onto the market and specializes in limited edition timepieces. Their current range includes the Bridges series.

Corum's emblem is a key pointing skywards and the company claims to have the "key to perfect time."

(left) Corum Bubble two-time zone, 1990s. Stainless steel, domed crystal.
*Courtesy of Antiquorum Auctioneers*

(above) Corum Bubble Swiss Flag, 2000s.
*Courtesy of Antiquorum Auctioneers*

(above) Corum Admiral's
Cup GMT 44, 2012.
*Courtesy of Antiquorum Auctioneers*

(right) Corum Spirit of
Ecstasy for Rolls Royce. 18K
white gold, 1980s.
*Courtesy of Antiquorum Auctioneers*

(above) Corum Trapezium
automatic. Stainless steel, 2000s.
*Courtesy of Antiquorum Auctioneers*

(right) Corum Bubble Casino
automatic, 2003.
*Courtesy of Antiquorum Auctioneers*

(below) Corum Twenty Dollar coin watch. 18K yellow gold, 1980s.

*Courtesy of Antiquorum Auctioneers*

(above) Corum Admiral's Cup diamond-set chronograph, 2010.

*Courtesy of Antiquorum Auctioneers*

(above) Corum Feather Dial, 1975. 18K white gold.
*Courtesy of Antiquorum Auctioneers*

(right) Corum Golden Bridge automatic. Titanium, visible movement, 2011.
*Courtesy of Antiquorum Auctioneers*

# *Croton*

Croton was founded in Switzerland in 1878. It has always been a highly innovative watch making company dedicated to offering desirable and affordable timepieces. The brand was acquired by Nationwide Time in 1991. Nationwide Time is a family-owned watch making business, established by the Mermelstein family in the 1960s. Since its acquisition, Croton has become increasingly focused on quality and now offers a lifetime warranty on all its movements. Croton sold one million watches in 2007. It is now a highly-recognized brand that describes itself as a "benchmark of quality, precision, style, and design."

Croton watches are now worn by many celebrities including Taylor Swift, Quincy Jones, and Josh Groban.

(left) Croton quartz with mineral crystal. Current model.

*Croton*

(above left) Croton quartz. Stainless steel, luminous hands. Current model.

*Croton*

(above middle) Croton quartz. Stainless steel, rubber strap. Current model.

*Croton*

(above right) Croton asymmetric dial. Stainless steel, leather strap. Current model.

*Croton*

(right) Croton Skeleton. Automatic, rectangular, current model.

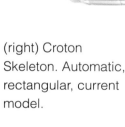

(right) Croton Aquamatic diver's watch. Large, stainless steel, date, current production.

(above left) Croton Tourbillon 3310. Rose gold, sapphire crystal. Current production.
*Croton*

(above right) Croton Tourbillon 3310. Yellow gold, sapphire crystal. Current production.
*Croton*

(below) Croton quartz. Blue dial and bezel. Current model.
*Croton*

(above) Croton quartz. Stainless steel, black and orange dial. Current production.
*Croton*

(left) Croton Chronomaster Aviator Sea Diver. Stainless steel, 1960s.
*Courtesy of Antiquorum Auctioneers*

111

# Cyma

Cyma was founded in 1862 by brothers Joseph and Theodre Schwob in the watch making town of Le Locle in Switzerland's Neuchatel region. Cyma is the French word for summit. From the outset the company produced technically brilliant timepieces that were noted for their resilience to temperature change, magnetism, and electricity. In its early years, the company produced around forty watches a day. The Schwob brothers formed a partnership with watchmaker Frederic Henri Sandoz in 1892, and the new enterprise built a factory at La Chaux-de-Fonds, Switzerland.

The company is still making watches. Cyma is now owned by Stelux International Limited, a Hong Kong-based holdings company.

(above) Cyma Cymaflex. Stainless steel. Ivory dial. Vintage.
*littlecogs.com*

(left) Cyma manual wind, hinged back.
*littlecogs.com*

(left) Cyma Oversize, 1920s. Silver

*Courtesy of Antiquorum Auctioneers*

(below) Cyma military, 1943. Stainless steel.

*littlecogs.com*

(above) Cyma chronometer, 1940s. Yellow gold.

*Courtesy of Antiquorum Auctioneers*

(below) Cyme Braille, vintage

*littlecogs.com*

(above left) Cyma concealed dial, 1950s.
*Courtesy of Antiquorum Auctioneers*

(above right) Cyma stainless steel square watch, 1950s.
*Courtesy of Antiquorum Auctioneers*

(above) Cyma gold-plated. Center seconds. Vintage.
*littlecogs.com*

(left) Cyma. Navystar Cymaflex. Gold-plated. Baton indexes. Center seconds. Vintage.
*littlecogs.com*

(left) Cyma. Gold-plated. White dial. Hinged back. Vintage.

*littlecogs.com*

# *Doxa*

Doxa was founded by Georges Ducommun in 1889. His company was located in the Jura region of Switzerland. In 1908 Doxa patented a movement with an eight-day power reserve. The company subsequently became closely involved with the motor industry when they began to manufacture dashboard instruments based on their eight-day movement. These were adopted by Bugatti. Doxa launched the first commercial diver's watch in 1968. The Doxa Sub had a distinctive orange dial and soon became a classic that is still in production.

(below) Doxa Staybrite chronograph, anti-magnetic. 1940s.
*Courtesy of Antiquorum Auctioneers*

(above) Doxa 14K pink gold, matte silver dial, 1950s.
*Courtesy of Antiquorum Auctioneers*

(below) Doxa Flyback chronograph. Large stainless steel watch, 1940s.
*Courtesy of Antiquorum Auctioneers*

(above) Doxa Le Locle steel chronograph, 1950.
*Courtesy of Antiquorum Auctioneers*

(below) Doxa 300 T Professional, 1976. Stainless steel diver's watch.
*Courtesy of Antiquorum Auctioneers*

(left) Doxa stainless steel with sun and moon display. 1960s.
*Courtesy of Antiquorum Auctioneers*

# Ebel

Ebel was founded in 1911 by Eugene Blum and his wife Alice Levy. Their company was located in Chaux-de-Fonds, Switzerland. The couple launched their first watch in 1912 and specialized in beautiful jeweled models. In the 1920s Ebel's Deco-style watches were very successful. During World War Two Ebel became an official supplier to the British Royal Air Force.

Ebel has developed many iconic watches during its century of production. The Videomatic was launched in 1952, the Chatelaine in 1954, the Sport Classic in 1977, the Chrono-Sport in 1982, the Discovery in 1984, the Beluga in 1985, and the Sportwave in 1997.

Ebel introduced its emblematic slogan the "Architects of Time" in the 1980s. The company stayed in the Ebel family until 2004 when it was acquired by the Movado Group. Brazilian model Gisele Bundchen is now the official face of Ebel.

(left) Ebel Classic 100, stainless steel, black alligator strap. Current production.

*Ebel*

(right) Ebel 1911 Discovery chronograph, stainless steel. Current model.

*Ebel*

(above) Ebel 18K yellow gold chronometer automatic, 1990s.

*Courtesy of Antiquorum Auctioneers*

(left) Ebel Antimagnetique chronograph 1940s.
*Courtesy of Antiquorum Auctioneers*

(below) Ebel 1911 Perpetual Calendar chronograph, 2006.
*Courtesy of Antiquorum Auctioneers*

(left) Ebel Le Modulor automatic chronograph, 1990s. 18K yellow gold and diamonds.
*Courtesy of Antiquorum Auctioneers*

(right) Ebel Voyager World Time, white gold 1990s.

*Courtesy of Antiquorum Auctioneers*

(below) Ebel 18K white gold, sapphire, and diamonds, 1964.

*Courtesy of Antiquorum Auctioneers*

(above) Ebel Classic Lady, stainless steel and 18K yellow gold. Current model.

*Ebel*

(below) Ebel Brasilia Mini, stainless steel. Current production.

*Ebel*

(above) Ebel Voyager World Time, stainless steel.

*Courtesy of Antiquorum Auctioneers*

# Eberhard

Georges-Emil Eberhard learnt his watch-making skills from his father. In 1887, he founded the Manufacture d'Horologie Eberhard et Compagnie in the Swiss town of La Chaux-de-Fonds. Eberhard specialized in precision timepieces and chronographs and soon built a reputation for excellence. In 1926 Georges-Emil's sons Georges and Maurice took over the business from their father. Their timepieces were adopted by the Italian Royal Navy in the 1930s and Eberhard also became closely involved with timing motor races. Their most famous watches include the Sirio of 1970, the Navymaster of 1987, the Tazio Nuvolari of 2001, the Chrono 4 of 2005, and the Scafodat diver's watch of 2006.

The company still produces up-dated versions of many of its most famous watches.

(left) Eberhard Aviograf.
Steel, late 1990s.
*Courtesy of Antiquorum Auctioneers*

(right) Eberhard Chrono 4
Temerario, 2006
*Courtesy of Antiquorum Auctioneers*

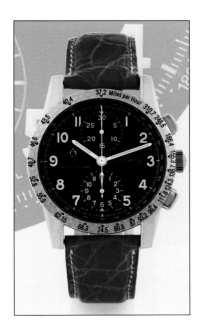

(above) Eberhard Tazio Nuvolari 1892 to 1982 Gold Car. 1992.
*Courtesy of Antiquorum Auctioneers*

(right) Eberhard Huit Jours. Over-sized stainless steel watch, 1990s.
*Courtesy of Antiquorum Auctioneers*

(below) Eberhard square button chronograph. 18K yellow gold, 1950s.
*Courtesy of Antiquorum Auctioneers*

# Elgin

Originally formed as the National Watch Company in 1864, Elgin was located in Chicago, Illinois. It was founded by a group of Chicago entrepreneurs including Chicago mayor Benjamin W. Raymond. The company moved to a new factory in Elgin, Illinois and changed its name to the Elgin National Watch Company in 1874. Elgin produced self-winding pocket watches and wrist watches and became very successful. The company switched to military production during the World War Two but recommenced civilian watch-making in the post-war years. The company relocated to South Carolina in 1964. Production ceased in 1968 and the Elgin name was sold. Chinese-produced watches are currently being marketed under the Elgin name.

 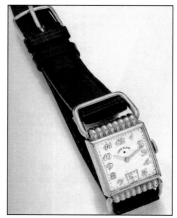

(above left) Elgin sterling silver, 1930s.
*Courtesy of Antiquorum Auctioneers*

(above right) Elgin 14K gold filled, 1940s.
*Courtesy of Antiquorum Auctioneers*

(right) Elgin cushion-shaped sterling silver, 1930s. Protective bezel.
*Courtesy of Antiquorum Auctioneers*

# *Eterna*

Swiss doctor Joseph Girard and teacher Urs Schild founded Eterna in 1856. Their inspiration was to bring employment to the Grenchen area of Switzerland. The company produced its first watch in the 1870s. The Eterna brand appeared in 1882 and launched the world's first wrist alarm clock in 1908. The Hexa self-winding sports watch appeared in the 1920s. The Eterna-matic movement was introduced in 1948 and the Golden Heart movement in the 1950s. Eterna introduced the trademark Kon-Tiki for its sports watches after Thor Heyerdahl's epic voyage across the Pacific Ocean. The Eterna Sonic appeared in 1970 and the Eterna quartz watch in 1974. Eterna launched the world's thinnest watch the Museum in 1980.

Professor Ferdinand Alexander bought Eterna in 1990. The company launched the Spherodrive movement in 2004. Eterna was bought by the Chinese company Haidian in 2011.

(below right) Eterna Adventic self-winding automatic, current model.

*Eterna*

(below) Eterna-matic with sweep seconds. 1960s.

*Trebor's Vintage Watches*

(below) Eterna Madison Eight Days. Spherodrive movement. Current model.

*Eterna*

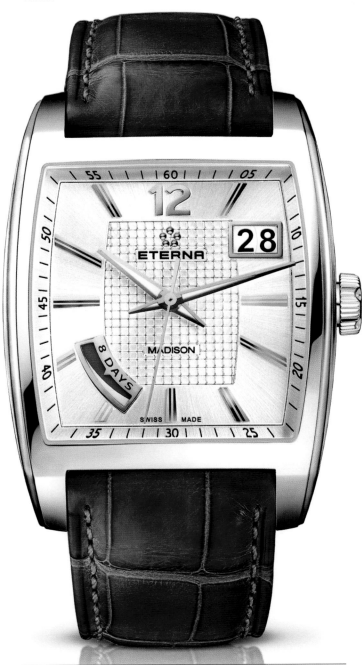

(below) Eterna Super Kon-Tiki 1973. Self-winding current model.
*Eterna*

(left) Eterna Kon-Tiki Date. Current model, self-winding.
*Eterna*

(below) Eterna automatic date.
*littlecogs.com*

(right) Eterna-matic with center seconds. Vintage watch.
*littlecogs.com*

(below) Eterna Pink gold Top. Vintage watch.
*littlecogs.com*

(above) Eterna Vaughan Big Date, current production. Stainless steel with anthracite dial.
*Eterna*

# Favre-Leuba

Swiss watchmakers Favre-Leuba was founded by Abraham Favre in 1718. The brand was registered in 1737 making it one of the oldest watchmakers in the world. The company stayed in the Favre family for eight generations, but is now in the process in being acquired by a subsidiary of the Tata Group of India. Favre-Leuba has launched many famous watches including the Bivouac in 1962, the Bathy in 1966, the Sea Raider in 1970, and the Mercury in 2003.

(above) Favre-Leuba stainless steel, automatic date, center seconds.

*littlecogs.com*

(left) Favre-Leuba Reverso, 1940s.

*Courtesy of Antiquorum Auctioneers*

(above) Favre-Leuba Moon Raider. Asymmetric, stainless steel, fiberglass, 1970s.

*Courtesy of Antiquorum Auctioneers*

(below) Favre-Leuba Bivouac, 1963. Altimeter and barometer.

*Courtesy of Antiquorum Auctioneers*

(above) Favre-Leuba Memo Raider, 1970s. Cushion-shaped.

*Courtesy of Antiquorum Auctioneers*

# Gallet

Gallet claims to be the oldest watchmaker in the world. The company was founded in Geneva, Switzerland in the fifteenth century. In 1895 Gallet became the first watch manufacturer to offer wrist-worn watches to the mass market for both men and women. Surprisingly these timepieces did not become popular until Gallet supplied wristwatches to soldiers in the World War One. Gallet introduced their famous Regulator and Duo Dial watches in 1927. In World War Two Harry S. Truman ordered a specially-designed Gallet wristwatch for the United States Air Force. The model was called the Flight Officer chronograph.

Bernard Gallet was the last member of the Gallet family to work in the company until his death in 2006. The company remains in private ownership.

(above) Gallet Flight Officer chronograph. 1940s.
*Courtesy of Antiquorum Auctioneers*

(right) Gallet stainless steel chronograph, 1930s.
*Courtesy of Antiquorum Auctioneers*

(below) Gallet steel chronograph, 1960s.
*Courtesy of Antiquorum Auctioneers*

# *Garrard*

Garrard & Company is a luxury jeweler founded by George Wickes in 1735. It was the British Crown Jewelers until 2007. For the last century, Garrard have made watches as part of their range.

(above Garrard stainless steel manual wind. Vintage watch.

*littlecogs.com*

(left) Garrard. Cushion-shaped. Center seconds, date window. Vintage.

*littlecogs.com*

(following page) Garrard 150th Anniversary watch. Limited edition, 1993. Made by Patek Philippe.

*Courtesy of Antiquorum Auctioneers*

# *Girard-Perregaux*

The original Girard-Perregaux business was started in Geneva, Switzerland in 1791 by master watchmaker Jean-Francois Bautte. The company was taken over by Constantin Girard and his wife Marie Perregaux in 1856. Girard-Perregaux made an early move away from pocket watches to wrist-worn timepieces. They were soon making watches for Kaiser Wilhelm's German naval forces. In 1928 the company was bought by Otto Graef. Under Graef's leadership, the company introduced a steady stream of famous models. These included the Sea Hawk in 1940, the Art Deco in 1945, and the Laureato in 1975. Luigi Macaluso took over Girard-Perregaux in 1992 and instigated productive partnerships with both Ferrari and the BMW Oracle yacht-racing team. One of the company's most extraordinary recent models is the Vintage 1945 Jackpot Tourbillon with its own tiny slot machine. Girard-Perregaux launched its Constant Escapement movement in 2008.

(above) Girard-Perregaux Sea Hawk II, dedicated to John Harrison, 2003.
*Courtesy of Antiquorum Auctioneers*

(left) Girard-Perregaux Retour en Vol chronograph, 2000.
*Courtesy of Antiquorum Auctioneers*

(above) Girard-Perregaux
Black Shadow. Ceramic
and titanium, 2010.
*Courtesy of Antiquorum*
*Auctioneers*

(above) Girard-Perregaux Ferrari
chronograph, 1990s.
*Courtesy of Antiquorum Auctioneers*

(left) Girard-Perregaux World
Time. White gold chronograph,
2007.
*Courtesy of Antiquorum Auctioneers*

(left) Girard-Perregaux BMW Oracle Fly-back chronograph.
*Courtesy of Antiquorum Auctioneers*

(below) Girard-Perregaux Richeville chronograph. 18K yellow gold, 1990s.
*Courtesy of Antiquorum Auctioneers*

# Glycine

Glycine was founded in 1914 by Eugene Meylan. The company was located in Bienne, Switzerland. Glycine specialized in excellent timepieces in beautiful jeweled cases. In 1934 Glycine launched a chronograph and followed this with a self-winding movement in 1945. Glycine introduced shock-resistant watches in 1952. The company's iconic Airman watch was launched in 1953. This was a mechanical aviation timepiece. The Airman range has been in continuous production since 1953 and Glycine continues to manufacture descendants of the original model.

Glycine struggled to survive the introduction of quartz movements in the 1970s, and the company was bought by Hans Brechbuhler in 1984. The company went on to introduce several famous models including the Goldshield, the Combat, and the Amaranth. Glycine says that is stands for both tradition and trend.

(right) Glycine Airman 18 Royal. Stainless steel and 18K red gold. Current production.

*Glycine Watch SA*

(below) Glycine Airman 7 Plaza Mayor Titanium. Current model.

*Glycine Watch SA*

(above) Glycine Steel Airman 7. Water-resistant, aviator's watch, 2002.

*Courtesy of Antiquorum Auctioneers*

(above) Glycine Airman Chrono 08. Stainless steel, current model.
*Glycine Watch SA*

(below) Glycine Stratoforte chronograph. Calf strap. Current model.
*Glycine Watch SA*

(above) Glycine Airman World Timer automatic. Stainless steel, circa 2000.
*Courtesy of Antiquorum Auctioneers*

(right) Glycine Ningaloo Reef chronograph. Sapphire glass, current production.

*Glycine Watch SA*

(below) Glycine Incursore automatic. Water-resistant, stainless steel, 1990s.

*Courtesy of Antiquorum Auctioneers*

(above) Glycine Airman 7 Crosswise self-winding, stainless steel. Current model.

*Glycine Watch SA*

(below) Glycine 18K white and yellow gold, rectangular. 1920s.

*Courtesy of Antiquorum Auctioneers*

(above) Glycine Incursore III. Automatic, stainless steel, black dial. Current model.

*Glycine Watch SA*

# *Gruen*

Dietrich Gruen was born in Germany and trained in Switzerland as a watchmaker. He immigrated to America as a young man and formed the Columbus Watch Manufacturing Company in 1876 based in Columbus, Ohio. The company produced watch cases, importing the movements from Switzerland. Dietrich and his son Frederick left the Columbus Watch Manufacturing Company and formed D. Gruen & Son. They launched the Veri-Thin line of watches in 1904. The company became very successful and grew to be the largest watchmaker in America. Dietrich Gruen died in 1911 and Frederick took over the business. He launched the Curvex model in 1935.

The Gruen family sold out of the business and it began to go into decline. It closed its doors in 1977.

(above) Gruen Precision autowind, 1960s.

*Trebor's Vintage Watches*

(right) Gruen Jump Hour Alpina. Sterling silver, ivory dial.

*Courtesy of Antiquorum Auctioneers*

(left) Gruen Curvex tank case, vintage watch.

*Trebor's Vintage Watches*

(below) Gruen square precision autowind. Early 1970s.

*Trebor's Vintage Watches*

(right) Gruen Alpina. Rectangular, stainless steel, silver dial, date.
*Courtesy of Antiquorum Auctioneers*

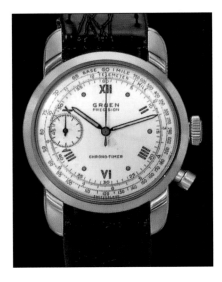

(above) Gruen Precision Chrono-Timer, 1950s. Mid-sized stainless steel watch.
*Courtesy of Antiquorum Auctioneers*

(below) Gruen Alpina 18K yellow gold rectangular watch. Movements 1930s, case 1980s.
*Courtesy of Antiquorum Auctioneers*

(above) Gruen 10K yellow gold-filled, 1940s.

*Courtesy of Antiquorum Auctioneers*

(right) Gruen Jump Hour Curvex. Nickel and pink gold-plated, 1950s.

*Courtesy of Antiquorum Auctioneers*

(below) Gruen Veri-Thin sweep second doctor's watch, 1930s.

*Trebor's Vintage Watches*

# *Gubelin*

The Gubelin business was founded by Jakob Josef Mauritz in Lucerne, Switzerland in 1854. As the business grew, Mauritz employed Eduard Jakob Gubelin as an apprentice. Gubelin subsequently married Mauritz's daughter and took over the business in 1899. The company is still a family business with Thomas Gubelin at its head.

(above) Gubelin concealed dial. 18K pink gold, 1940s.
*Courtesy of Antiquorum Auctioneers*

(right) Gubelin 18K pink and white gold two-tone baguette, circa 1935.
*Courtesy of Antiquorum Auctioneers*

(far right) Gubelin white and yellow gold. Square Art Deco, 1930.
*Courtesy of Antiquorum Auctioneers*

(left) Gubelin stainless steel manual wind and center seconds.

*littlecogs.com*

---

(right) Gubelin Staybrite Reverso. Pink gold, 1932.

*Courtesy of Antiquorum Auctioneers*

---

(below) Gubelin concealed dial. Yellow gold and diamonds, 1950s.

*Courtesy of Antiquorum Auctioneers*

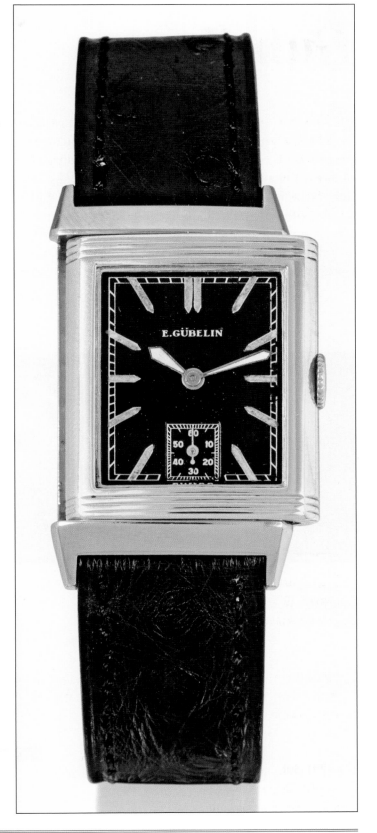

# Hamilton

Hamilton was founded in 1892 in Lancaster, Pennsylvania. From the beginning Hamilton focused on modernity in both its technology and styling. The company manufactured watches and navigational equipment, launching its first watch in 1893. The Yankee watch appeared in 1928. In the 1930s Hamilton became an official supplier of precision equipment to the airlines, including Eastern, TWA, Northwest, and United. During World War II, Hamilton produced over one million military watches, including the Khaki series. In the 1950s Hamilton watches made their first movie appearance in "The Frogmen." Hamilton introduced the first electric watch in 1957. In 1961 Elvis Presley wore a Hamilton Ventura in the film "Blue Hawaii." The company launched the Pulsar in 1970 and the Pan Europ in 1971.

In 2003 Hamilton transferred their headquarters to Biel, Switzerland. Hamilton watches are now Swiss made, combining American spirit with Swiss precision.

(above) Hamilton Pan Europ automatic, center seconds. Vintage.

*littlecogs.com*

(right) Hamilton swing lug diver's watch. Yellow gold-filled, 1940s.

*Trebor's Vintage Watches*

(far right) Hamilton tank case. 18K yellow gold, 1940s.

*Trebor's Vintage Watches*

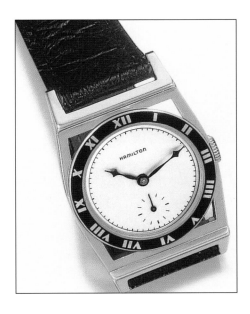

(left) Hamilton Pulsar Digital. Cushion-shaped LED quartz, 1972.

*Courtesy of Antiquorum Auctioneers*

(above) Hamilton Piping Rock. 14K yellow gold tonneau-shaped, 1950s.

*Courtesy of Antiquorum Auctioneers*

(below) Hamilton slim profile, manual wind. Stainless steel, 1960s.

*Trebor's Vintage Watches*

(right) Hamilton vintage military watch. Hack seconds, 1940s.

*Trebor's Vintage Watches*

(left) Hamilton Chronomatic Fontaine-bleu. Stainless steel monocoque, 1950.

*Courtesy of Antiquorum Auctioneers*

(above) Hamilton 14K white gold and diamonds, 1940.

*Courtesy of Antiquorum Auctioneers*

(left) Hamilton Jazz Master. Steel split-second chronograph, 2008.

*Courtesy of Antiquorum Auctioneers*

(above) Hamilton Khaki automatic chronograph. Oversized, 2008.

*Courtesy of Antiquorum Auctioneers*

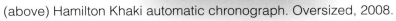

(right) Hamilton platinum and diamonds. Concealed dial, 1950s.

*Courtesy of Antiquorum Auctioneers*

(left) Hamilton Ventura Electric. Asymmetrical center seconds. 14K yellow gold, 1960.
*Courtesy of Antiquorum Auctioneers*

(below) Hamilton Ventura Electric. Asymmetrical, 14K yellow gold, 1957.
*Courtesy of Antiquorum Auctioneers*

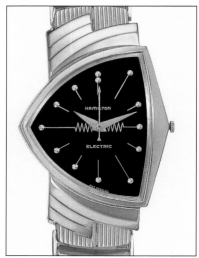

(above) Hamilton Otis. Rectangular, 14K yellow gold-filled, 1950s.
*Courtesy of Antiquorum Auctioneers*

# Harwood Watch Co.

Harwood was established by Englishman John Harwood. He was the inventor of the Harwood automatic watch movement, which he patented in Switzerland in 1924. The Harwood Perpetual watch was launched two years later. John Harwood had developed a highly unusual timepiece without a winding crown. Instead the watch is wound and the hands are adjusted by a rotating bezel. Harwood believed that this would prevent moisture getting into the watch through the crown aperture. In modern Harwoods, a small red control indicator shows if the watch is in operational or adjusting mode.

The company's reputation grew quickly. In 1929, Lady Drummond Hay timed the round-the-world voyage of the airship Count Zeppelin with her Harwood wristwatch. In 2004 Princess Carolin of Monaco was photographed wearing her Harwood watch.

The Harwood Watch Co. is now based at Grenchen in Switzerland and Peter Harwood is the chief operating officer of the company.

(left) Harwood. Stainless steel, leather strap. White dial. Current.
*Hardwood Watch Co.*

(right) Harwood. Square, silver case. Ivory dial, luminous hands. No crown.
littlecogs.com

(above) Harwood self-winding. Stainless steel, tonneau-shaped. 1920s.

*Courtesy of Antiquorum Auctioneers*

(above) Harwood stainless steel. Fluted revolving bezel. 2000.

*Courtesy of Antiquorum Auctioneers*

(right) Harwood sterling silver. Tonneau-shaped. Self-winding. Late 1920s.

*Courtesy of Antiquorum Auctioneers*

(far left) Harwood. Stainless steel, diamond-set bezel. Current.

*Hardwood Watch Co.*

(left) Harwood Louis Reguin enamel dial. Limited edition, available in steel or platinum. Current.

*Hardwood Watch Co.*

(above) Harwood. Limited edition, sterling silver. Winding bezel. Current.

*Hardwood Watch Co.*

(below) Harwood stainless steel. Black dial, white hands. Current.

*Hardwood Watch Co.*

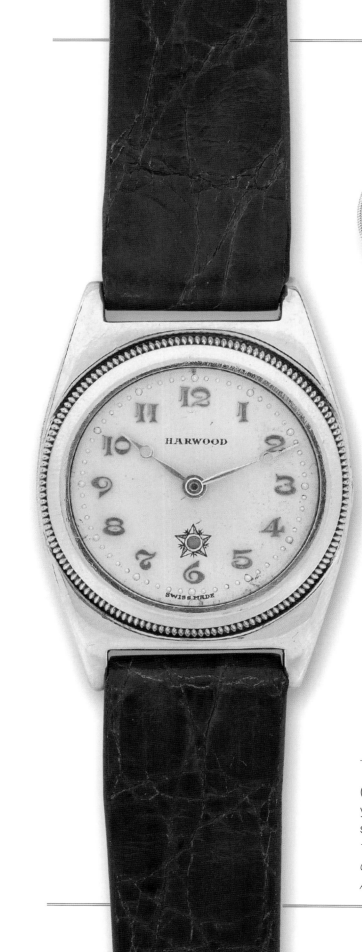

(left) Harwood stainless steel and gold. Revolving gold bezel. 2000.
*Courtesy of Antiquorum Auctioneers*

(below) Harwood. 18K yellow gold. Commemorates the eightieth anniversary of Harwood's patent. Current.
*Hardwood Watch Co.*

(right) Harwood. Center seconds, winding bezel. Stainless steel, integral bracelet. Current model.
*Hardwood Watch Co.*

(right) Harwood hexagonal-shaped. Gold-plated. Self-winding. Hand-set indicator. 1920s.
*Courtesy of Antiquorum Auctioneers*

(left) Harwood 18K yellow gold. Tonneau-shaped. Self-winding. 1930s.
*Courtesy of Antiquorum Auctioneers*

# *Helbros*

Helbros was founded in 1913 by the Swiss-German Helbein brothers. The company name was a truncation of Helbein Brothers. From the beginning Helbros manufactured inexpensive watches for the masses. Many of their watches were branded with promotional logos and were used in marketing. Their technical high point came in the 1960s when they designed a watch that told lunar time. The S & S Time Corporation of Tulsa, Oklahoma is now the exclusive distributor for Helbros in the United States.

(above) Helbros. White and yellow gold-filled. Three-dimensional numerals. Vintage.

(below) Helbros gold-filled tonneau case, ribbon lugs. 1940s.

*Trebor's Vintage Watches*

(above) Helbros. Diamond-set, manual wind. Vintage.

(right) Helbros Invincible. Stainless steel, manual wind. 1960s.

# Heuer

Edouard Heuer founded this prominent watch making brand in 1860 at the age of twenty. He located his new business in St. Imier, Switzerland. Heuer launched his first chronograph in 1882 and these timepieces became the focus of the business. In 1887 Heuer invented the oscillating pinion movement which is still in use today. Heuer launched a repeater watch with automatic chiming in 1888, a water-resistant case in 1895, and Pulsometer dials in 1908. Heuer began to manufacture dashboard chronographs in 1911 and women's wristwatches in 1912.

Heuer manufactured the first wrist-worn chronographs in 1914, sports chronometers in 1920, pilot's chronographs in 1930, and water-resistant chronographs in 1939.

Heuer timepieces have been worn by many famous people. General Eisenhower bought a Heuer watch in 1945 and Steve McQueen wore several Heuer watches. Lewis Hamilton is a current devotee of the brand.

Heuer introduced many iconic models during the twentieth century. These included the Auto-Graph in 1948, the Solunar in 1949, the Mareograph in 1950, the Mikrotimer in 1966, and the Chronosplit Manhattan GMT in 1977. Their twenty-first century models have included the titanium Kirium T15 in 2000, the Monaco Sixty Nine in 2003, the V4 Concept in 2004, the Professional Golf Watch in 2005, and the Caliber S in 2007.

In 1985, Heuer joined the TAG group and changed their company name to Tag-Heuer. Jack Heuer remains as the company's honorary chairman. Heuer is now the fourth largest prestige watch brand in the world. The company slogan is the "Swiss Avant-Garde since 1860."

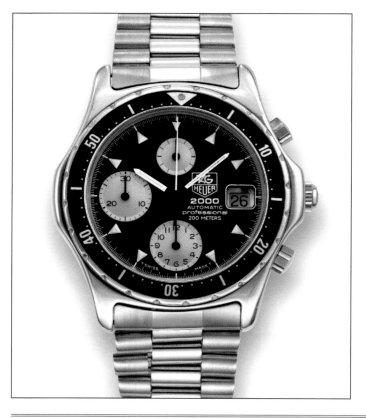

(left) Heuer Professional automatic. Stainless steel, 1990s.
*Courtesy of Antiquorum Auctioneers*

(right) Heuer Carrera Caliber 1887. Stainless steel 2012.
*Courtesy of Antiquorum Auctioneers*

(left) Heuer chronometer. 18K yellow gold, 1910.

*Courtesy of Antiquorum Auctioneers*

(below) Heuer Monaco Python chronograph. Spare python strap, 2007.

*Courtesy of Antiquorum Auctioneers*

(left) Heuer 2000 Collection. Steel and 18K yellow gold, 2000.

*Trebor's Vintage Watches*

(below) Heuer stainless steel chronograph, 1950s.

*Courtesy of Antiquorum Auctioneers*

(above) Heuer Monaco self-winding automatic chronograph, 1972.

*Courtesy of Antiquorum Auctioneers*

(left) Heuer automatic tonneau-shaped chronograph, 1970s.

*Courtesy of Antiquorum Auctioneers*

(below) Heuer Kentucky automatic. Stainless steel and yellow gold, 1977.

*Courtesy of Antiquorum Auctioneers*

(left) Heuer Carrera vintage chronograph, 1960s.

*Trebor's Vintage Watches*

(left) Heuer Verona automatic chronograph.
Stainless steel and yellow gold, 1979.
*Courtesy of Antiquorum Auctioneers*

(above) Heuer Calculator. Oversized, tonneau-shaped automatic
chronograph, 1970s.
*Courtesy of Antiquorum Auctioneers*

(left) Heuer Monaco Gulf Edition. Limited edition automatic
chronograph, 2007.
*Courtesy of Antiquorum Auctioneers*

(below) Heuer Monaco Steve McQueen. Square, convex automatic chronograph. Stainless steel, 1970.

*Courtesy of Antiquorum Auctioneers*

(right) Heuer Autavia chronograph. 18K pink gold, 2003.

*Courtesy of Antiquorum Auctioneers*

(right) Heuer Camaro. 18K yellow gold, tonneau-shaped chronometer, 1965.

*Courtesy of Antiquorum Auctioneers*

(above) Heuer Leonidas Carrera. Stainless steel chronograph, late 1960s.

*Courtesy of Antiquorum Auctioneers*

(left) Heuer Silverstone. Antimagnetic, automatic chronograph, 1974.

*Courtesy of Antiquorum Auctioneers*

(above) Heuer Jack Heuer Carrera.
Limited edition, 1964.
*Courtesy of Antiquorum Auctioneers*

(right) Heuer Solunar automatic. High and
low tide indicators, 1960s.
*Courtesy of Antiquorum Auctioneers*

(right) Heuer 100 Meters. 18K yellow gold, quartz, 1980s.
*Courtesy of Antiquorum Auctioneers*

(below) Heuer Diamond Dial Professional Line, 2000s.
Rotating bezel.
*Courtesy of Antiquorum Auctioneers*

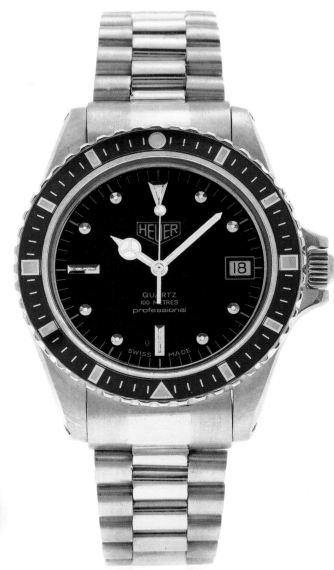

(left) Heuer Monza chronograph. Black ebonite and stainless steel, 1970s.
*Courtesy of Antiquorum Auctioneers*

(right) Heuer Carrera chronograph. Salmon and silver dial, circa 2000.
*Courtesy of Antiquorum Auctioneers*

# IWC *International Watch Company*

IWC was founded in 1868 by the American watchmaker Florentine Ariosto Jones. Although Jones learned his watch making craft in Boston, Massachusetts he located his company in Schaffhausen, Switzerland. Jones built his factory on the banks of the river Rhine. IWC has produced several iconic models including the Pilot's watch in 1936 and the Portuguese in 1939. IWC manufactured many pilots' watches during World War II. These included the W. W. W. of 1944 (this stood for watch, wrist, waterproof). The company went on to launch the Aquatimer in 1967, the Da Vinci in 1969, and the Ingenieur in 1976.

IWC was taken over by Richemont in 2000. The company continues to manufacture most of its iconic ranges as well as Porsche sport watches. IWC also manufactures the most complicated watch in the world the Il Destriero Scafusia.

(left) IWC Big Pilot's watch. Current.
*IWC*

(right) IWC manual wind. 18K rose gold, circa 1950.
*Trebor's Vintage Watches*

(below) IWC pink gold chronograph.
*IWC*

(left) IWC Da Vinci
automatic with big date.
Current model.
*IWC*

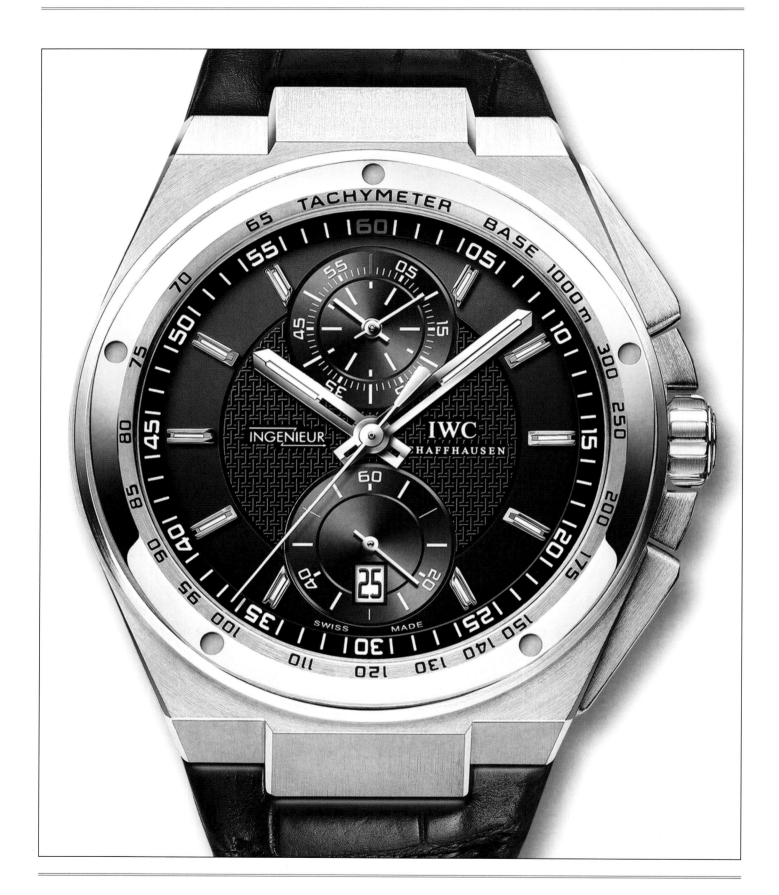

(right) IWC GST automatic chronograph. Stainless steel, circa 2000.
*Courtesy of Antiquorum Auctioneers*

(below) IWC Ingenieur. Tonneau-shaped, anti-magnetic, circa 1990.
*Courtesy of Antiquorum Auctioneers*

(above) IWC Aquatimer self-winding chronograph, rotating bezel. Current production.
*IWC*

(left) IWC Big Ingenieur chronograph. Pellaton automatic winding system. Current model.
*IWC*

(right) IWC Portuguese Chronograph
Rattrapante. 18K yellow gold, 1990s.
*Courtesy of Antiquorum Auctioneers*

(below IWC Electronic. Stainless steel,
1980s.
*Courtesy of Antiquorum Auctioneers*

(right) IWC Staybrite stainless steel, 1970s.
*Courtesy of Antiquorum Auctioneers*

(left) IWC. Stainless steel. Center seconds. Vintage.

*littlecogs.com*

(below) IWC Da Vinci perpetual calendar chronograph. 18K yellow gold, late 1990s.

*Courtesy of Antiquorum Auctioneers*

(right) IWC automatic. Center seconds. Vintage.

*littlecogs.com*

(left) IWC Portuguese Skeleton F. A. Jones. Oversized, platinum, 2005.
*Courtesy of Antiquorum Auctioneers*

(above) IWC Novecento perpetual automatic. Rectangular, platinum, 1990s.
*Courtesy of Antiquorum Auctioneers*

(left) IWC automatic. Square, stainless steel, 1970s.
*Courtesy of Antiquorum Auctioneers*

# Jaeger-LeCoultre

LeCoultre was founded by Antoine LeCoultre in 1835. The company claims to be the first watchmaker to have built a factory in Switzerland's famous Joux Valley. LeCoultre soon won a reputation for making accurate and dependable timepieces. The enterprise launched over five-hundred different calibers and complications, including two-hundred chronographs.

Watchmaker Edmond Jaeger set up his watch making business in Paris, France in 1880. He was the official supplier of watches to the French navy. Jaeger met Antoine LeCoultre's grandson Jacques-David LeCoultre in 1925 and the pair soon formed a partnership. Although the luxury goods trade was depressed, the new partnership launched the world's smallest watch movement (the Caliber 101) in

1929. Jaeger-LeCoultre soon began to develop a range of iconic models. The Reverso appeared in 1931, the Memovox in 1950, the Futurematic in 1953, the Geophysic in 1958, and the Master Mariner diving watch in 1967. The company also formed working partnerships with other prestigious companies including Ferrari and Aston Martin supplying timepieces and movements.

Jaeger-LeCoultre is still based in Le Sentier, Switzerland just yards from the original factory. The Jaeger-LeCoultre museum was opened in Le Sentier in 2009. The company is now part of the Richemont luxury goods group. Jaeger-LeCoultre continues to develop its famous models including the Atmos and Memovox. The Reverso is the company's most popular watch.

(left) Jaeger-LeCoultre Master Memovox. Stainless steel, alarm, 2012.
*Courtesy of Antiquorum Auctioneers*

(above) Jaeger-LeCoultre engraved skeleton. 18K yellow gold, 1980s.
*Courtesy of Antiquorum Auctioneers*

(left) Jaeger-LeCoultre Reverso Grande GMT. Small seconds hand. Current production.

*Jaeger-LeCoultre*

(right) Jaeger-LeCoultre Reverso Grande Sun Moon. Twin-barrel movement, current model.

*Jaeger-LeCoultre*

(above) Jaeger-LeCoultre Grande Reverso Duodate. Day/night indicator, current model.

*Jaeger-LeCoultre*

(left) Jaeger-LeCoultre Reverso Geographique. Limited edition, 18K pink gold, 1999.

*Courtesy of Antiquorum Auctioneers*

(above) Jaeger-LeCoultre Polaris II Deep Diver Alarm Memovox GT. 1960s.
*Courtesy of Antiquorum Auctioneers*

(left) Jaeger-LeCoultre Mystery. Tonneau-shaped, 18K white gold, 1970s.
*Courtesy of Antiquorum Auctioneers*

(above) Jaeger-LeCoultre 18K
yellow gold, manual wind.
Circa 1960.

*Trebor's Vintage Watches*

(above) Jaeger-LeCoultre Amvox II Aston Martin.
Titanium chronograph, 2008.

*Courtesy of Antiquorum Auctioneers*

(right) Jaeger-LeCoultre automatic. Reserve power
indicator. Gold-filled, vintage.

*littlecogs.com*

(left) Jaeger Steel Reverso. Stainless steel, rectangular, reversible. 2004.

*Courtesy of Antiquorum Auctioneers*

Jaeger-LeCoultre. Rectangular, steel. Baton indexes. Vintage.

*littlecogs.com*

(below) Jaeger-LeCoultre manual wind, center seconds, alarm. Gold-filled, vintage.

*littlecogs.com*

(left) Jaeger-LeCoultre Polaris. Automatic, stainless steel, mechanical alarm. Circa 1960s.
*Courtesy of Antiquorum Auctioneers*

(left) Jaeger-LeCoultre cushion-shaped, white gold and diamonds. Textured mesh bracelet, 1970s.
*Courtesy of Antiquorum Auctioneers*

(right) Jaeger-LeCoultre Extreme World Chronograph Valentino Rossi 46. Limited edition, oversized, 18K pink gold and titanium. 2006.
*Courtesy of Antiquorum Auctioneers*

(below) Jaeger-LeCoultre. Gold dial, baton indexes. Center seconds. Vintage.

*littlecogs.com*

(above) Jaeger-LeCoultre Pulsations chronograph. 1990s.

*Courtesy of Antiquorum Auctioneers*

(right) Jaeger-LeCoultre doctor's chronograph. 18K pink gold, 1940s.

*Courtesy of Antiquorum Auctioneers*

(right) Jaeger-LeCoultre. Rectangular, manual wind. 10K gold-filled, subsidiary seconds. Vintage.

*littlecogs.com*

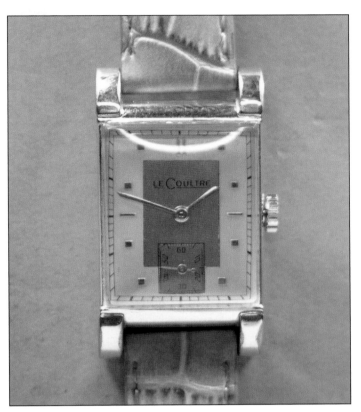

(right) Jaeger-LeCoultre Powermatic automatic. 10K gold-filled. Circa 1950.

*littlecogs.com*

# Jules Jurgensen

Jules Jurgensen and his partner Isaac Larpent established a watch-making business in Copenhagen, Denmark in 1740. The company can claim to be one of the world's oldest watchmakers. In the early years, the business made chronometers for the Royal Danish government. Jules Jurgensen's grandson Jules opened a branch of the company in Switzerland while his great-grandson Louis Urban Jurgensen managed the Danish part of the business. Jules Jurgensen watches were produced in Switzerland until 1957. The brand was sold to the American businessman Mort Clayman in 1974. His company assembled competitively-priced watches from imported parts.

(below) Jules Jurgensen Urban Tourbillon. Minute repeater, platinum, 2004.
*Courtesy of Antiquorum Auctioneers*

(above) Jules Jurgensen. Tonneau-shaped 18K yellow gold, five-minute repeater, circa 1920.
*Courtesy of Antiquorum Auctioneers*

(above) Jules Jurgensen Chronograph 20
ATM. Tonneau-shaped, stainless steel,
1960s.

*Courtesy of Antiquorum Auctioneers*

(right) Jules Jurgensen Urban Jurgensen.
Self-winding, 18K pink gold, moon phases,
1990s.

*Courtesy of Antiquorum Auctioneers*

# *Juvenia*

Juvenia was founded in 1860 by Jacques Didisheim. The company was first located at St. Imier, Switzerland but Didisheim soon re-located to the famous watch making village of La Chaux-de-Fonds. Juvenia was a diverse manufacturing company producing watches, jewelry, motors, and spectacles among other things. Gradually Juvenia started to manufacture its own watch movements. They were keen to export their products and were one of the first watchmakers to gain access to the developing Chinese market. Juvenia watches are still produced at La Chaux-de-Fonds in Switzerland but the company is now owned by Asia Commercial Holdings of Hong Kong. The company slogan "Divine Inspiration" was introduced in 2005. Notable current models include the Biarritz, Classique, and Planet.

(left and above) Juvenia Planet. 18K pink gold, circa 1995.
*Courtesy of Antiquorum Auctioneers*

(above right) Juvenia 1860. Water-resistant, 18K yellow gold, 1990s.
*Courtesy of Antiquorum Auctioneers*

(above left) Juvenia Astronomic. Automatic, stainless steel and yellow gold-plated. 1953.

*Courtesy of Antiquorum Auctioneers*

(above right) Juvenia Architecture. 10K gold-filled, 1950s.

*Courtesy of Antiquorum Auctioneers*

(left) Juvenia large chronograph. Pink gold, 1940s.

*Courtesy of Antiquorum Auctioneers*

(right) Juvenia automatic. 18K yellow gold, Florentine-style bezel. 1960.

*littlecogs.com*

# Longines

Longines has been based at St. Imier, Switzerland since 1832. The business was founded by Auguste Agassiz. It began with craftspeople assembling watches in their homes. When Agassiz became ill his nephew Ernest Francillon took over the company in 1854. Francillon had a more industrial approach to watch making and built a factory on a piece of land known as Les Longines in St. Imier. By 1911 the Longines factory employed over a thousand workers.

The company introduced the winged hourglass logo in 1867 which remains unchanged to this day. Their company motto is "Precision, Elegance." Longines had become the official timekeeper for many sports events including the Royal Ascot horserace in England and the French Tennis Championships. By 2000 Longines had manufactured over thirty million watches and the brand is now sold in over one-hundred-and-thirty countries. Longines is now owned by the Swatch Group, the world's leading watch producer. Walter von Kanel is the company president.

Longines has appointed several Ambassadors of Elegance including Andre Agassi, Stephanie Graf, and Kate Winslet.

(below) Longines Sport Admiral. Stainless steel, sapphire crystal. Current production.
*Longines*

(above) Longines manual wind. Subsidiary seconds, snap back. Circa 1940.
*littlecogs.com*

(right) Longines Prima Luna. 18K pink gold, date. Current model.

*Longines*

(below) Longines Grande Vitesse chronograph. Stainless steel, automatic, 2012.

*Courtesy of Antiquorum Auctioneers*

(right) Longines Heritage chronograph. Stainless steel, silver dial, alligator strap. Current production.

*Longines*

(right) Longines automatic. Waterproof, antimagnetic, shock resistant. Stainless steel. Vintage.

*littlecogs.com*

(below) Longines Lindbergh Hour Angle. Stainless steel and yellow gold, 1987.
*Courtesy of Antiquorum Auctioneers*

(right) Longines manual wind. Stainless steel. Circa 1948.
*littlecogs.com*

(above) Longines 9K yellow gold. Subsidiary seconds. Circa 1948.
*littlecogs.com*

(left) Longines manual. Stainless steel, center seconds. Circa 1955.

*littlecogs.com*

(below) Longines Mysterious. White gold and diamonds. 1950s.

*Courtesy of Antiquorum Auctioneers*

(below) Longines manual wind. Subsidiary seconds, snap back. Vintage.

*littlecogs.com*

(above) Longines Sport Hydroconquest chronograph. Stainless steel, blue aluminum bezel. Current model.

*Longines*

(above) Longines diver's chronograph. Tonneau-shaped, stainless steel, 1969.

*Courtesy of Antiquorum Auctioneers*

(right) Longines manual wind. Stainless steel. Circa 1959.

*littlecogs.com*

(below) Longines Steel Evidenza automatic chronograph, 2000s.
*Courtesy of Antiquorum Auctioneers*

(above) Longines manual-wind. Subsidiary seconds, vintage.
*littlecogs.com*

(below) Longines Olympian Calendar automatic. 14K yellow gold-capped over steel. 1972.

(left) Longines Saudi Arabia. Pink gold-plated, 1960.
*Courtesy of Antiquorum Auctioneers*

(below) Longines Gold Flyback chronograph. 18K pink gold, 1950s.
*Courtesy of Antiquorum Auctioneers*

(left) Longines. Gold. Subsidiary seconds. Vintage.

*littlecogs.com*

(below) Longines manual-wind. Stainless steel, snap back, vintage.

*littlecogs.com*

(below) Longines 18K yellow gold. Limited edition, circa 2000.

*Courtesy of Antiquorum Auctioneers*

(right) Longines. Gold-plated. Rectangular, decorative lugs. Subsidiary seconds. Vintage.

*littlecogs.com*

(above) Longines medical chronograph. Large, 18K pink gold, 1960.
*Courtesy of Antiquorum Auctioneers*

(left) Longines Weems aviator's wristwatch. Large, Staybrite stainless steel, 1930s.
*Courtesy of Antiquorum Auctioneers*

(right) Longines manual-wind. Stainless steel, snap back, vintage.

*littlecogs.com*

(above) Longines 1492 Christobal C. Solar compass, hinged bezel, wind names. 1992.

*Courtesy of Antiquorum Auctioneers*

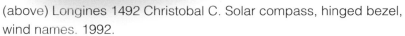

(right) Longines automatic. Center seconds, screw back, vintage.

*littlecogs.com*

(left) Longines manual wind.
Stainless steel, 1956.

*littlecogs.com*

(below) Longines manual-wind.
Stainless steel, screw back, vintage.

*littlecogs.com*

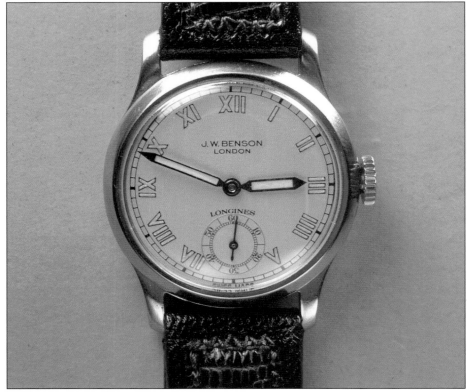

(left) Longines stainless steel.
Subsidiary seconds. Circa 1934.

*littlecogs.com*

(left) Longines Evidenza automatic. Tonneau-shaped, stainless steel, self-winding. Current production.

*Longines*

(above) Longines Retour en Vol chronograph. Staybrite stainless steel, register, tachometer. 1942.

*Courtesy of Antiquorum Auctioneers*

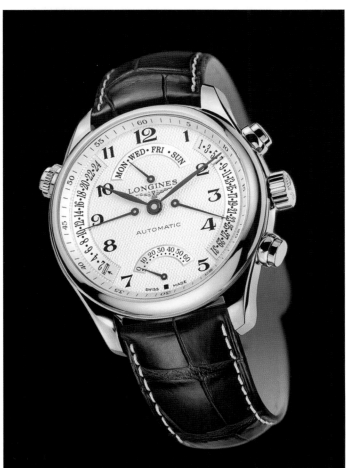

(left) Longines Master. 18K pink gold, water-resistant, barleycorn-pattern dial. Current model.

*Longines*

(above) Longines automatic. 9K yellow gold. Center seconds. Circa 1960.

*littlecogs.com*

(right) Longines Master Collection GMT. Automatic, stainless steel, 2005.

*Courtesy of Antiquorum Auctioneers*

(left) Longines manual-wind. Stainless steel, subsidiary seconds, snap back. Vintage.

*littlecogs.com*

# *Mappin*

Mappin & Webb can trace its roots back to 1774 when Jonathan Mappin began his silversmiths business in Sheffield, England. His descendant John Newton Mappin developed a successful electroplating and cutlery company. As the business grew, Mappin formed a partnership with his brother-in-law George Webb. The company became Mappin & Webb in 1868. The business had a large showroom in London and began to commission and retail jewelry and watches. Mappin & Webb is now the official silversmith to both Queen Elizabeth II and the Prince of Wales. The company is owned by the Jewelers Goldsmiths group.

(above) Mappin automatic, center seconds, screw back. 1962.
*littlecogs.com*

(above) Mappin rectangular silver case. Subsidiary seconds. 1930.
*littlecogs.com*

# Marvin

Marvin was founded by Marc and Emmanuel Didisheim in 1850. The company was located in St. Imier in Switzerland's watch making Jura region. The Marvin brand was registered in Berne, Switzerland in 1893. Marvin was always innovative and Marc Didisheim's son registered seventeen new patents between 1891 and 1911. The company moved to the famous watch making town of La Chaux-de-Fonds in 1894. In the early years Marvin had assembled watches using some parts made by other companies but from 1912 the company manufactured all of its own components.

Marvin fell into financial difficulties in the quartz revolution of the 1970s and the brand was bought by an Italian company. The company became independent once more in 2002 and launched its new model line in 2007.

(above) Marvin manual wind, subsidiary seconds. 520 caliber. Vintage.

*Littlecogs disc*

(left) Marvin M120 Sellita SW200 movement. See-through case back. Current production.

*Marvin Watch Co.*

(below) Marvin M121 Loeb chronograph. ETA Valjoux 7750 movement. Current model.

*Marvin Watch Co.*

(left) Marvin Flying Hour. Rectangular, stainless steel. Ronda 751 and 753 movements. Current production.

*Marvin Watch Co.*

(above) Marvin M115 Dubois-Depraz movement. Stainless steel,
regulator. Current model.

*Marvin Watch Co.*

(below) Marvin automatic. Felsa
690 caliber. Stainless steel,
vintage.

*Littlecogs disc*

# *Mido*

Mido was founded by Swiss watchmaker Georges Schaeren in 1918. The company made Deco-style models in the 1920s. In the 1930s they based several iconic watches on the radiator grilles of prestige automobiles including Bugattis, Buicks, and Chevrolets. Mido launched the Multifort anti-magnetic watch in 1934. Several famous models followed. These included the Powerwind in 1954, the monocoque Ocean Star in 1959, the Baroncelli in 1976, the Worldtimer and the Bodyguard (complete with security alarm) in 1995, and the Belluna in 2008.

Bjorn Borg became Mido's spokesperson in 1981. The company motto is "Reflection on Time." Mido is now part of the Swatch Group.

Mido automatic. PVD-coated steel. Anti-reflective crystal. Current model.
*Mido*

Mido convertible brooch/bracelet watch. 18K pink gold and diamonds. 1950s.
*Courtesy of Antiquorum Auctioneers*

Mido Moonphase. Large, stainless steel, automatic. Current model.
*Mido*

# MIDO

(right) Mido Diver. Automatic, stainless steel.
Current production.
*Mido*

(below) Mido Ettore Bugatti. 18K white and
yellow gold, late 1930s.
*Courtesy of Antiquorum Auctioneers*

(right) Mido Multifort.
Super Automatic,
Powerwind. 14K
yellow gold, late
1950s.
*Courtesy of Antiquorum
Auctioneers*

(below) Mido Belluna
Lady. Screwed crown,
stainless steel and
diamonds. Current
model.
*Mido*

# Military Watches

Being able to know the time is vitally important in all theatres of combat, on the battlefield, at sea, or in the air. Early military wristwatches were adapted from pocket watches by attaching two soldered lugs either side of the watch. Two leather straps were then fitted to the lugs so that the watch could be worn on the wrist. This made it much easier to read the time in action. In 1879 the German Kaiser ordered more than a thousand military watches from the Swiss watchmaker Girard-Perregaux of Geneva. These timepieces were probably the first military watches to be commissioned in bulk by a military authority. The Girard-Perregaux watches were originally ordered to supply the Imperial German navy but the idea soon caught on in the other military services.

Men in civilian life had been slow to accept the idea of wearing a wristwatch. Before the war, these were considered a fashion item for women. Most men still preferred to use a traditional pocket watch. But during the World War I many military personnel started to wear military watches on home leave. This led to wristwatches being seen as both manly and fashionable.

As World War II approached, military authorities worldwide increased their acquisition of military watches. The Japanese government commissioned thousands of watches from Seiko. The Germans government ordered watches from IWC (the Swiss-based International Watch Company), and the German watchmaker A. Lange & Sohne. The British military authorities placed their orders with Swiss companies Jaeger-LeCoultre, Omega, and Movado. The American government ordered watches from American companies Bulova, Hamilton and Waltham.

Aviators also soon realised the importance of an accurate timepiece. The first pilot's watch was introduced by IWC around 1936. It was a large faced military watch with a rotating glass bezel. It was fitted with a small caliber pocket watch movement.

The most important military watch function was the hack feature. Hacking is when the watch allows the second hand to be stopped (via the winding crown) to synchronize timing. This allowed military personnel to synchronise their military watches with split second precision.

Military watches continued to be issued by various military authorities during the Cold War years. Combatants in the Vietnam War, the Gulf conflict, and the wars in Iraq and Afghanistan have all been issued with military timepieces. Military-style watches have now also become very popular with the general public and are manufactured by a wide range of watchmakers. The rugged good looks of military watches have been translated into tough and often complicated timepieces for civilian wear and are now on the cutting-edge of fashion.

## British Military Watches

(below) Buren military watch.

*www.militarywatchbuyer.com*

(left) British Army Issue Pulsar watch.

*www.militarywatchbuyer.com*

(below left) Cyma military wristwatch.

*www.militarywatchbuyer.com*

(below) CWC (Cabot Watch Company) British Army-issue timepiece.

*www.militarywatchbuyer.com*

(left) Hamilton army-issue wristwatch.

*www.militarywatchbuyer.com*

(below) Eberhard 1900 British Army-issue pocket watch. Swiss-made.

*www.militarywatchbuyer.com*

(above) Jaeger-LeCoultre WWW (waterproof wristlet watch).

*www.militarywatchbuyer.com*

(right) Lemania WWW.

*www.militarywatchbuyer.com*

(below) Longines WWW.

*www.militarywatchbuyer.com*

(right) Vertex WWW.
*www.militarywatchbuyer.com*

(above) Smiths British army-issue watch.

*www.militarywatchbuyer.com*

(right) Lemania Fleet Air Arm chronograph.
Series 1.

*www.militarywatchbuyer.com*

(below) Lemania Fleet Air Arm chronograph.

*www.militarywatchbuyer.com*

(above) CWC (Cabot Watch Company) Royal Navy
diver's watch.

*www.militarywatchbuyer.com*

(above) Hamilton RAF chronograph.

*www.militarywatchbuyer.com*

(right) IWC Mark II RAF timepiece.

*www.militarywatchbuyer.com*

(below) Omega WWW.

*www.militarywatchbuyer.com*

(right) Omega 1956 RAF-issue wristwatch.

*www.militarywatchbuyer.com*

(right) RAF aircrew Hamilton wristwatch.

www.militarywatchbuyer.com

(above) Omega 1953 RAF-issue timepiece.

www.militarywatchbuyer.com

(right) RAF-issue Newmark chronograph.

www.militarywatchbuyer.com

(right) Jaeger-LeCoultre
RAF-issue Mark II.

*www.militarywatchbuyer.com*

(left) IWC Mark 11 RAF-
issue watch.

*www.militarywatchbuyer.com*

(above) RAF Longines.
1956.

*www.militarywatchbuyer.com*

(right) Omega 1956.
RAF-issue wristwatch.

*www.militarywatchbuyer.com*

(left) Seiko first generation RAF-issue watch.

*www.militarywatchbuyer.com*

___

(right) RAF-issue Omega.

*www.militarywatchbuyer.com*

(above) Seiko second generation RAF quartz chronograph.

*www.militarywatchbuyer.com*

___

(right) RAF Omega.

*www.militarywatchbuyer.com*

___

(left) Hanhart Luftwaffe pilot chronograph.

*www.militarywatchbuyer.com*

## German Military Watches

(below) Hanhart Luftwaffe pilot chronograph.

*www.militarywatchbuyer.com*

(above) Arsa vintage German army watch.

*www.militarywatchbuyer.co*

(above) Hanhart Luftwaffe pilot watch.

*www.militarywatchbuyer.com*

(right) German artillery chronograph pocket watch.

*www.militarywatchbuyer.co*

(above) Heuer post-war Luftwaffe chronograph.
*www.militarywatchbuyer.com*

(left) A. Lange & Sohne Luftwaffe observer's watch.
*www.militarywatchbuyer.com*

(right) Luftwaffe Tutima pilot's chronograph.
*www.militarywatchbuyer.com*

# *American Military Watches*

(below) Hamilton United States Army watch.

*www.militarywatchbuyer.co*

(above) Benrus watch issued during the Vietnam War.

*www.militarywatchbuyer.co*

(below) American Air Force A11 military wristwatch.

*www.militarywatchbuyer.co*

(left) Elgin watch issued to the United States army ordinance department.

*www.militarywatchbuyer.co*

(below) American Air Force ADNAC wristwatch.

*www.militarywatchbuyer.co*

# *Movado*

Achilles Ditesheim opened his watch making workshop with six craftsmen in 1881. His business was located in the Swiss watch making village of Chaux-de-Fonds. Ditesheim chose Movado as his trademark in 1905. This innovative company has launched many successful wristwatches. Their models included the curved Polyplan in 1912, the Digital (with numeric hours and minutes) in 1930, the Calendomatic in 1946, the single dot dial Museum in 1947, the Kingmatic in 1956, and the gold coiled cuff watch favored by Elizabeth Taylor in 1960. Movado launched the Datron in 1970, the Vizio in 1996, the Elliptica in 2001, the Strato in 2005, the Series 800 in 2006, the Master in 2009, and the Bold in 2010.

Movado was bought by the North American Watch Corporation in 1983. Movado continues to produce updated versions of their iconic models. They also manufacture watches for premium brands such as Coach, Lacoste, and Tommy Hilfiger.

(right) Movado World Time. 18K yellow gold, ridged bezel. 1950.

*Courtesy of Antiquorum Auctioneers*

(below) Movado 18K pink gold. Manual wind, subsidiary seconds, vintage.

*littlecogs.com*

(above) Movado Master.
Oversized tonneau-shaped,
stainless steel. Current model.
*Movado*

(below) Movado Sport. Stainless
steel. Vintage.
*littlecogs.com*

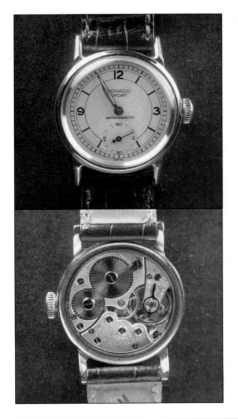

(above) Movado. Gold-plated. Subsidiary seconds, date. Vintage.
*littlecogs.com*

(left) Movado chronograph. Date, day, month indicators. Subsidiary seconds. Vintage.

*littlecogs.com*

(below) Movado stainless steel chronograph. 1960.

*Courtesy of Antiquorum Auctioneers*

(above) Movado 18K white gold and diamonds. 1960s.

*Courtesy of Antiquorum Auctioneers*

(right) Movado manual wind. 9K yellow gold. Center seconds, snap back. 1955.

*littlecogs.com*

(above) Movado Bold. Swiss quartz movement. Current model.

*Movado*

(right) Movado automatic. Yellow gold. Vintage.

*littlecogs.com*

(left) Movado manual wind. 9K yellow gold. Center seonds, snap back. 1950.

*littlecogs.com*

(right) Movado Vizio. Tungsten carbide bezel, date. Automatic quartz chronograph. Current production.

*Movado*

(above) Movado Series 800. Unidirectional bezel, date. Current production.

*Movado*

(left) Movado automatic. 9K yellow gold. Center seconds, snap back. Circa 1948.

*littlecogs.com*

(above)
Movado
manual wind.
Stainless steel,
snap back.
Vintage.
*littlecogs.com*

(above) Movado subsidiary seconds. Stainless steel. Vintage.
*littlecogs.com*

(right) Movado automatic. Stainless steel, date. Vintage.
*littlecogs.com*

(right) Movado Calendomatic automatic.
Stainless steel, day/month indicators.
Circa 1952.

*littlecogs.com*

(below) Movado Zenith. Thin,
hexagonal, 14K yellow gold. 1970s.
*Courtesy of Antiquorum Auctioneers*

(above) Movado 9K gold. Manual wind, subsidiary seconds.
1950.
*littlecogs.com*

(right) Movado chronometer. Moon phases, date, day, months. Luminous hands. Vintage.

*littlecogs.com*

(below) Movado Triple Calendar. 18K pink gold, moon phases. 1940s.

*Courtesy of Antiquorum Auctioneers*

(right) Movado center seconds. Date. Vintage.

*littlecogs.com*

(above) Movado
Andy Warhol Times
Five. Limited edition,
1988.
*Courtesy of Antiquorum*
*Auctioneers*

# *Omega*

Omega holds several world records for accuracy and is one of the world's most successful watchmakers. The company began in 1848 when Louis Brandt set up his Louis Brandt & Son workshop in Switzerland's La Chaux-de-Fonds. Brandt originally assembled watches from parts made by local craftspeople. In 1879 he switched to manufacturing his own parts and built a factory. Brandt launched the Labrador watch in 1885. The Omega trade name was suggested to Brandt in 1903 by banker Henri Rieckel. Omega launched its first waterproof watches in 1937 and its first automatic watch in 1943. The company went on to develop many iconic watches. These included the Seamaster in 1948, the Constellation in 1952, the Speedmaster in 1957, and the De Ville in 1960. The Marine Chronometer followed in 1974,

and the Hour Vision in 2007.

NASA chose the Speedmaster Professional as its official timepiece in 1965 and the Apollo XI astronauts wore Speedmasters on the 1969 moon mission. The Omega worn by Neil Armstrong is the only watch in the world to have been worn on the surface of the moon. Speedmaster watches were also worn by the Russian and American astronauts of the 1975 Apollo-Soyuz mission.

Omega opened its famous museum in Bienne, Switzerland in 1984. The company was quick to pick up on the fashion for vintage wristwatches, and launched Omega Vintage Watches in London's Burlington Arcade in 2007.

Omega's ambassadors include Nicole Kidman, Ellen McArthur, and George Clooney.

(left) Omega Constellation. Stainless steel chronometer, 1958.
*Courtesy of Antiquorum Auctioneers*

(below) Omega Constellation. 18K white gold, automatic, tonneau-shaped chronometer. 1968.
*Courtesy of Antiquorum Auctioneers*

(above left) Omega Turler. 18K yellow gold, 1949.
*Trebor's Vintage Watches*

(above right) Omega Grand Sport automatic. Gold-plated, 1969.
*Trebor's Vintage Watches*

(above) Omega Constellation. Red gold chronometer. Current model.
*Omega*

(right) Omega manual wind. Stainless steel, vintage.
*littlecogs.com*

(left) Omega Constellation. White gold and diamonds. Omega 8401 movement. Current production.
*Omega*

(right) Omega Bumper Automatic. Stainless steel chronometer, 1958.

*Trebor's Vintage Watches*

(below) Omega Dynamic TV Case. Automatic, stainless steel, day/date. Circa 1970.

*Courtesy of Antiquorum Auctioneers*

(above) Omega. Rectangular, stainless steel. Subsidiary seconds. Vintage.

*littlecogs.com*

(above left) Omega Co-Axial Chronoscope. Palladium and diamonds. Omega 3313 movement. Current model.

*Omega*

(above right) Omega Olympic Timeless. White gold. Current production.

*Omega*

(above) Omega Cosmos. 18K yellow gold, textured bracelet. 1960.

*Courtesy of Antiquorum Auctioneers*

(left) Omega Second Generation Flightmaster. Two time zone aviator's watch. 1973.

*Courtesy of Antiquorum Auctioneers*

(above) Omega Planet Ocean
chronograph. Helium escape valve.
Current model.

*Omega*

(above) Omega Planet Ocean Orange
Co-Axial. Diver's chronometer, 2008.

*Courtesy of Antiquorum Auctioneers*

(right) Omega Planet Ocean
Chronograph. Stainless steel and
diamonds. Helium escape valve.
Current production.

*Omega*

# OMEGA

(above) Omega chronometer. Stainless steel and diamonds. Omega 3313 movement. Current model.

*Omega*

(left) Omega De Ville. Diamonds and rubies, 18K yellow gold. Oval, quartz, 2000.

*Courtesy of Antiquorum Auctioneers*

(below) Omega De Ville Dynamic. Automatic, horizontal oval, stainless steel, day/date. 1970s.

*Courtesy of Antiquorum Auctioneers*

(left) Omega De Ville. 9K yellow gold, manual wind. 1977.

*littlecogs.com*

Omega Speedmaster Professional Snoopy Award. Commemorates 1970 Apollo X11 mission. 2003.
*Courtesy of Antiquorum Auctioneers*

(below) Omega Speedmaster Schumacher.
Asymmetric, stainless steel. 2002.

*Courtesy of Antiquorum Auctioneers*

(above) Omega Speedmaster. Automatic, stainless steel,
asymmetric. Self-winding, circa 1996.

*Courtesy of Antiquorum Auctioneers*

(left) Omega. 9K yellow gold Dennison case.
Vintage.

*littlecogs.com*

(above) Omega Golden Nugget. 18K yellow
gold bracelet. 1960.

*Courtesy of Antiquorum Auctioneers*

(left) Omega. Gold. Center seconds, date.
Vintage.

*littlecogs.com*

# OMEGA

(above) Omega Jewelry. 18K white gold and diamonds, integrated bracelet. 1960s.

*Courtesy of Antiquorum Auctioneers*

(below) Omega. Gold-plated, stainless steel back. Waterproof. Vintage.

*littlecogs.com*

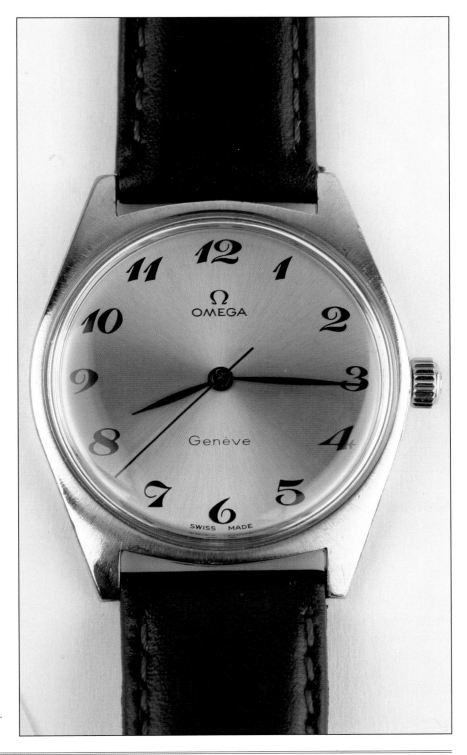

(above) Omega Seamaster automatic. Gold, stainless steel back. Vintage.

*littlecogs.com*

(right) Omega Seamaster. Automatic, stainless steel, asymmetric. Self-winding, circa 1996.

*Courtesy of Antiquorum Auctioneers*

(left) Omega Big Blue Seamaster. Automatic chronograph. Omega shark bracelet. 1972.
*Courtesy of Antiquorum Auctioneers*

(below) Omega Seamaster 600 Ploprof. Automatic, asymmetric, stainless steel. 1970s.
*Courtesy of Antiquorum Auctioneers*

(left) Omega Museum chronograph. Manual-wind, white gold. Limited edition. Current model.
*Omega*

(right) Omega Seamaster chronometer. Electronic. Center seconds. Vintage.

*littlecogs.com*

(above) Omega Seamaster. 14K yellow gold, automatic. Vintage.

*littlecogs.com*

(right) Omega Seamaster automatic. Stainless steel. Date. Vintage.

*littlecogs.com*

(below) Omega Marine. Rectangular, midsized. Staybrite stainless steel, 1930s.

*Courtesy of Antiquorum Auctioneers*

(above) Omega Railmaster Aqua Terra XXL. Oversize chronometer. Mother-of-pearl, diamonds, and stainless steel. 2005.

*Courtesy of Antiquorum Auctioneers*

(right) Omega automatic. Stainless steel. Center seconds, date. Vintage.

*littlecogs.com*

(above) Omega Dynamic. Horizontal oval, stainless steel, date. 1960s.

*Courtesy of Antiquorum Auctioneers*

(right) Omega stainless steel. Center seconds. Vintage.

*littlecogs.com*

# *Oris*

Oris proudly asserts that it makes "purely mechanical" watches. The company's distinctive red rotor symbolizes their proud mechanical tradition. Oris was founded in 1904 by Paul Cattin and Georges Christian in Holstein, Switzerland. The company is still based in its original buildings. Oris has close connections with motor racing, aviation, diving, movies, and music. The company has made several timepieces commemorating famous musicians including Dizzy Gillespie, Duke Ellington, Frank Sinatra, Bob Dylan, and Louis Armstrong. Oris also sponsors Formula One motor racing and launched its first Chronoris motor racing watch in the 1970s. The company is the partner of the AT&T Williams Formula One racing team.

Oris launched its first Pointer Day aviator's watch in the 1940s. The company sponsors the Swiss Hunter Team a group of former Swiss Air Force pilots who fly a range of legendary aircraft.

Oris watches have appeared in many movies, worn by Sean Connery, Meg Ryan, Julianne Moore, Gwyneth Paltrow, Harrison Ford and many other Hollywood stars.

Oris's company slogan is "Real watches for real people."

(left) Oris Bob Dylan, limited edition. Rectangular, stainless steel, automatic, date. Current model.
*Oris*

(left) Oris Kittiwake. Limited edition diver's watch. Titanium, automatic. Current model.

*Oris*

(right) Oris Raid 2011 Chronograph. Stainless steel, limited edition. Current production.

*Oris*

(above) Oris automatic. Date, center seconds, screw back. Vintage.

*littlecogs.com*

(left) Oris Classic Tonneau Regulator. Automatic, gold-filled. 1990s.

*Courtesy of Antiquorum Auctioneers*

(above) Oris stainless steel and gold plate. Water-resistant. 2008.

*Courtesy of Antiquorum Auctioneers*

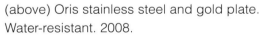

(right) Oris Steel TT1 diver's watch. Stainless steel, Oris link bracelet. 2003.

*Courtesy of Antiquorum Auctioneers*

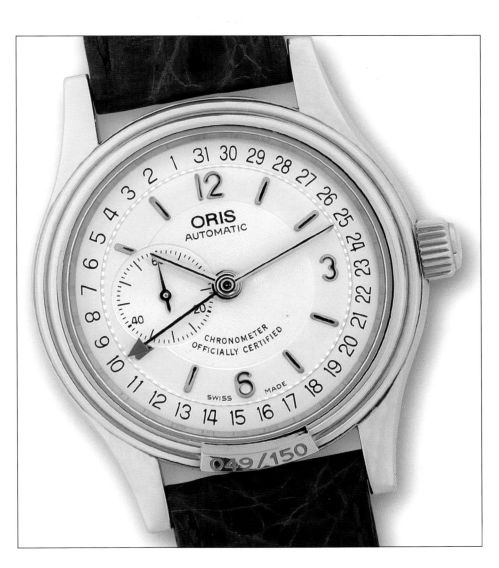

(above and right) Oris Gold
Chronometer. Limited edition. 18K
pink gold. 2000.

*Courtesy of Antiquorum Auctioneers*

(left) Oris Louis Armstrong. 18K gold
chronometer, date. 2001.

*Courtesy of Antiquorum Auctioneers*

(above) Oris Classic Date. Stainless steel, big crown, automatic. Superluminova C3 hands. Current production.

*Oris*

(below) Oris Swiss Hunter Team PS Edition. Stainless steel aviator's watch. Current production.

*Oris*

(left) Oris Pink Gold Worldtimer. Chronometer, 18K pink gold. 2000.

*Courtesy of Antiquorum*

*Auctioneers*

(above) Oris Williams F1 Team
Skeleton Engine Date. Stainless steel,
fine timing device. Current model.
*Oris*

(below) Oris Steel Worldtimer
Centennial. Two time zones,
day/night indicator. 2004.
*Courtesy of Antiquorum Auctioneers*

(left) Oris Artelier
Worldtimer. Water-
resistant, stainless
steel, two time
zones. 2000.
*Courtesy of Antiquorum
Auctioneers*

# *Panerai*

Panerai was established in 1860 by Giovanni Panerai. His shop was located in Florence, Italy. From the beginning the company specialized in timepieces and other precision mechanisms. Panerai soon became a supplier to the Royal Italian navy. The company supplied the navy with all kinds of underwater instruments, underwater torches, wrist compasses, and wrist depth gauges. More importantly they also developed their iconic Radiomir underwater watch for naval use. Guido Panerai developed the first luminescence in 1910 and patented this important invention. His achievement is celebrated by the company's Luminor models. Panerai introduced their first two automatic watches in 1998. These were the Luminor Submersible diver's watch and the Luminor GMT. In recent year Panerai has become famous for its very large and robust sports chronometers. Many of these watches have Panerai's security-lever-protected crown.

Panerai's flagship store is still located in Florence's Piazza San Giovanni, but the company is now owed by the Swiss luxury goods group Richemont. Celebrity Panerai wearers include the artist Damien Hirst, Arnold Schwarzenegger, Ben Affleck, Sylvester Stallone, and Brad Pitt.

(left) Panerai Luminor 112. Limited edition. Large, cushion-shaped. Stainless steel. 2012.
*Courtesy of Antiquorum Auctioneers*

(above) Panerai Luminor 1950 GMT automatic. Ceramic. 47mm special edition. 2012.
*Courtesy of Antiquorum Auctioneers*

(right) Panerai Ferrari Chrono Rattrapante. Limited edition. Stainless steel. 2008.
*Courtesy of Antiquorum Auctioneers*

(right) Panerai
Luminor Submersible
1950 automatic.
Bronze. 47mm
special edition. 2012.
*Courtesy of Antiquorum*
*Auctioneers*

(above) Panerai Radiomir. Pink gold. 2006.
*Courtesy of Antiquorum Auctioneers*

(left) Panerai Luminor GMT automatic. Military diver's
watch. Large, cushion-shaped. Stainless steel. 2008.
*Courtesy of Antiquorum Auctioneers*

(right) Panerai Luminor Power Reserve. Stainless steel.
2002.
*Courtesy of Antiquorum Auctioneers*

(left and below) Panerai Luminor Marina 1950. Three days power reserve. 47mm special edition. 2012.

*Courtesy of Antiquorum Auctioneers*

(right and below) Panerai Radiomir 1940 Oro Rosso. 47mm special edition. 2012.

*Courtesy of Antiquorum Auctioneers*

(above) Panerai Luminor Automatic Chrono. Crown with security lever. Stainless steel. 2001.

*Courtesy of Antiquorum Auctioneers*

# *Patek Philippe*

In 1839 two Polish immigrants to Switzerland (Antoni Patek and Francois Czapek) founded a watch making company in Geneva. Swiss watchmaker Jean-Adrien Philippe joined the company in 1844. Czapek left the business a year later and it was renamed Patek Philippe & Cie. in 1851. From the beginning Patek Philippe was an innovative and technically advanced watchmaker. It created the first wristwatch in 1867. The Patek Philippe wristwatch was adopted by Queen Victoria and became hugely popular. The company went on to patent a perpetual calendar mechanism in 1889 and a split-seconds chronograph in 1902.

Patek Philippe was acquired by the Stern family in 1932 and is now one of the oldest family-owned watch making companies in the world. Thierry Stern became company president in 2009. Under this stable leadership, Patek Philippe has become well known for its creativity and inventiveness. The company has launched several iconic watch lines including the Calatrava in 1932, the Ellipse in 1968, the Nautilus sports watch in 1976, and the Gondolo in 1993.

The Patek Philippe Museum was opened in Geneva, Switzerland in 2001. Its collection is dedicated to five centuries of watch making.

(above) Patek Philippe Caliber 5000. Rose gold. Copper sunburst dial. Current model.

(left) Patek Philippe Officer's Watch. Military-style bezel and crown. Breguet numerals.

(below) Patek Philippe Perpetual Calendar automatic. Ultra-thin. 18K yellow gold.

(below) Patek Philippe platinum with diamond and emerald markers. Bought in Lima, Peru. 1949.

(left) Patek Philippe  Gondolo  Annual Calendar watch. 18K yellow gold. 2011.

(above, left and below) Patek Philippe 5216R Grand Complications. Tourbillon, rose gold. Moon phases.

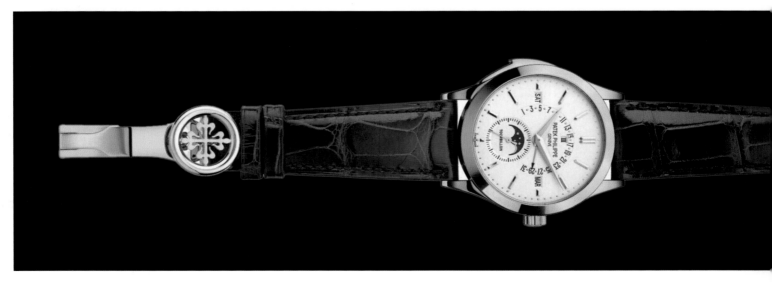

(left) Patek Philippe Calatrava. 18K yellow gold. Current model.

(right) Patek Philippe Celestial 5106. 2009.

(below) Patek Philippe Tropical cloisonné dial. 1954.

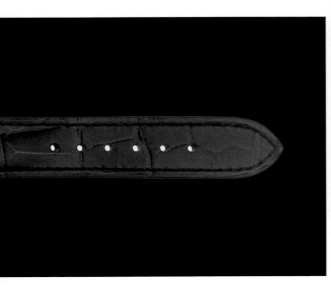

(left) Patek Philippe. Square. Stainless steel and pink gold. 1954.
*Courtesy of Antiquorum Auctioneers*

(below) Patek Philippe Jump Date. 18K yellow gold. Self-winding. 1962.
*Courtesy of Antiquorum Auctioneers*

(above) Patek Philippe bracelet watch. Floral
enamel dial. Platinum and diamonds. 1914.

*Courtesy of Antiquorum Auctioneers*

(above) Patek Philippe Golden Ellipse. Ultra-thin, platinum. Current.

*Patek Philippe*

(above) Patek Philippe Retrograde Perpetual Calendar. 18K white gold, moon phases. 2008.

*Courtesy of Antiquorum Auctioneers*

(right) Patek Philippe. Oval. White gold and diamonds. 1979.

*Courtesy of Antiquorum Auctioneers*

(below) Patek Philippe
Complications World Time.
White gold. Current.
*Patek Philippe*

(above and right) Patek
Philippe Complications
Skeleton. White gold,
small-linked bracelet.
Current.
*Patek Philippe*

Patek Philippe Gondolo Chronometer.
18K yellow gold, 1911.
*Courtesy of Antiquorum Auctioneers*

(left) Patek Philippe
Nautilus Titanium.
2007

(above) Patek Philippe Nautilus black dial. 1990s.

(left) Patek Philippe Nautilus Chrono.

(below) Patek Philippe Luminous Dial. 18K yellow
gold. Twenty-four-hour indication. 1992.

*Courtesy of Antiquorum Auctioneers*

(above) Patek Philippe.
Horizontal, elliptical.
18K white gold. 1974.
*Courtesy of Antiquorum
Auctioneers*

(above) Patek Philippe Ellipse
d'Or. 18K yellow gold, integral
bracelet. Agate and mother-of-
pearl dial. 1977.
*Courtesy of Antiquorum Auctioneers*

(right) Patek Philippe. Oval.
White gold and diamonds.
Fine woven-link bracelet.
1973.
*Courtesy of Antiquorum Auctioneers*

(right) Patek Philippe Jumbo Aquanaut. Cushion-shaped, stainless steel, date. 2009.
*Courtesy of Antiquorum Auctioneers*

(left) Patek Philippe Neptune. Yellow gold, link bracelet. Quartz, 1990s.
*Courtesy of Antiquorum Auctioneers*

(right) Patek Philippe Calatrava. 18K yellow gold, Breguet numerals. 1952.
*Courtesy of Antiquorum Auctioneers*

(right) Patek Philippe First Series.
Yellow gold. Perpetual calendar,
moon phases, chronometer, register,
tachometer. 1948.
*Courtesy of Antiquorum Auctioneers*

(below) Patek Philippe Tiger Eye.
18K yellow gold and tiger eye
bangle watch. Rectangular, tiger
eye dial. 1985.
*Courtesy of Antiquorum Auctioneers*

(left) Patek Philippe World Time. 18K white gold. Guilloche silver dial. 2002.

*Courtesy of Antiquorum Auctioneers*

(above and right) Patek Philippe Only Watch. Tourbillon, Breguet-style numerals. Stainless steel, sapphire crystal case back.

*Courtesy of Antiquorum Auctioneers*

(left) Patek Philippe. 18K white gold. Wide, textured bezel. 1960.

*Courtesy of Antiquorum Auctioneers*

(above and left) Patek Philippe concealed dial. 18K white gold and diamonds. 1968.

*Courtesy of Antiquorum Auctioneers*

(right) Patek Philippe. 18K yellow gold, subsidiary seconds. Stepped bezel. 1950s.

*Courtesy of Antiquorum Auctioneers*

(left) Patek Philippe manual wind. 18K yellow gold, 1965.

*Trebor's Vintage Watches*

(below) Patek Philippe Steel Aquanaut.
Stainless steel, date. Produced between
1997 and 2006.
*Courtesy of Antiquorum Auctioneers*

(above) Patek Philippe Nautilus. Brushed
stainless steel and 18K yellow gold. Flat
bezel. 1992.
*Courtesy of Antiquorum Auctioneers*

# Piaget

Georges Edouard Piaget founded his watch making company in 1874. It was located in his home village of La Cote-aux-Fees in Switzerland's Jura Mountains. His assembled watches became famous for their fusion of luxury materials and precision movements. Piaget's motto was "Always do better than necessary." The Piaget brand name was officially registered in 1943 as the company began to manufacture its own movements. Piaget launched the Emperador watch in 1957 and the company diversified into jewelry-making in the same year. Piaget had a creative flowering in the 1960s and 1970s, introducing many unusual timepieces. These were both highly decorative and extremely accurate, and fitted with increasingly thin movements. The company's range included the flamboyant cuff watch, precious-stone-dial watches, and several new model lines. Piaget's Polo watch came out in 1979 followed by the Dancer range in 1986. Piaget watches were adopted by many high profile celebrities of the period including Jackie Kennedy, Gina Lollobrigida, and Andy Warhol.

Piaget became part of the Richemont luxury goods group in 1988. A succession of new watches was launched in the 1990s including the Possession, the ultra-thin Altiplano, the Tanagra, the Limelight, and the Miss Protocole. Piaget also created the world's thinnest tourbillon movement in 2002, the Caliber 600P.

Piaget's headquarters are now in Geneva, Switzerland. The company has a high profile in the world of the performing arts and has been a major sponsor of the elite game of polo since the 1970s. Many of Piaget's iconic model lines are still in production.

(above) Piaget Altiplano automatic. Ultra-thin. Subsidiary seconds. 18K yellow gold. Current.

(above) Piaget Altiplano manual wind. Rose gold.

(right) Piaget Limelight Twice, two separate movements. Haute Joaillerie Limelight Twice. Diamond-set sunburst dial.

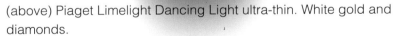

(above) Piaget Limelight Dancing Light ultra-thin. White gold and diamonds.

(right) Piaget Protocole 18K white gold and diamonds.

(left) Piaget Altiplano Double Jeu. Mechanical. 18K yellow gold.

(right) Piaget Limelight Garden Party. 18K pink gold and diamonds, concealed dial. Mother-of –pearl case and slide.

(below) Piaget Dancer ultra-thin. White gold and diamonds.

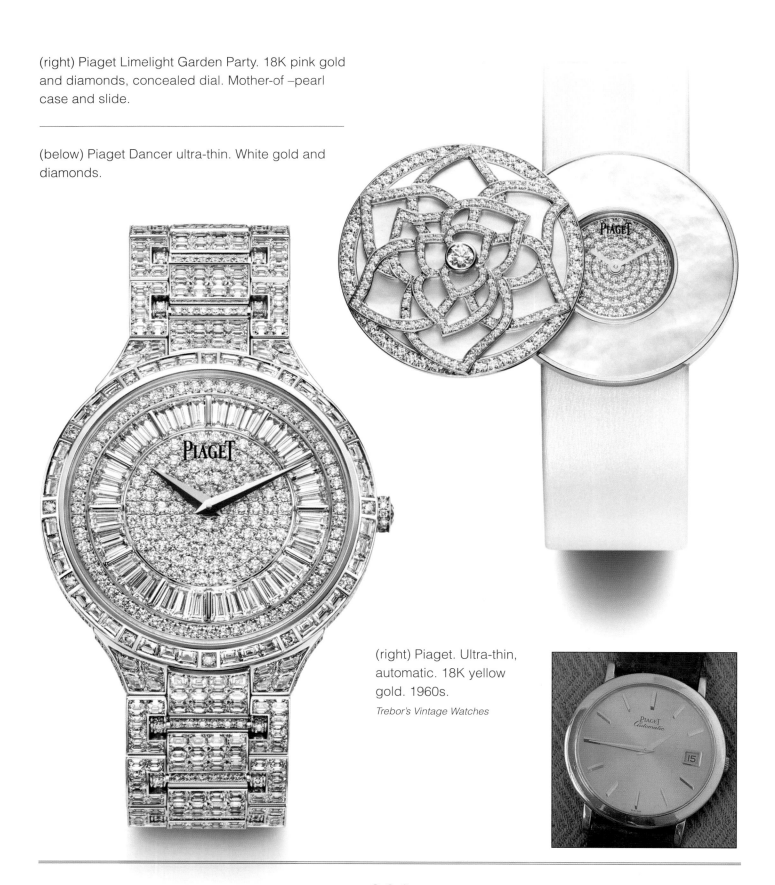

(right) Piaget. Ultra-thin, automatic. 18K yellow gold. 1960s.

*Trebor's Vintage Watches*

(left) Piaget Limelight Dancing. 18K white gold and diamonds. Revolving rose, concealed dial.

(below) Piaget Altiplano automatic. Classic styling. 18K yellow gold, baton indexes. Current.

(above) Piaget Altiplano square mechanical watch. 18K yellow gold.

(left) Piaget Altiplano Fingerprint. White gold and brilliant-cut diamonds.

*Courtesy of Antiquorum Auctioneers*

(below) Piaget Dual Time Zone. 18K yellow gold. Two movements. 1970s.
*Courtesy of Antiquorum Auctioneers*

(above) Piaget oval. White gold and diamonds, textured bracelet. 1990s.
*Courtesy of Antiquorum Auctioneers*

(left) Piaget Rose Limelight Garden Party secret dial. 18K white gold and diamonds. Current.

(below) Piaget Limelight Magic Hour. Quartz. 18K white gold and diamonds. Rotating bezel.

(right) Piaget Dual Time Zone Flyback Chronograph. Titanium and steel. 2008.

*Courtesy of Antiquorum Auctioneers*

(above) Piaget tri-color gold and diamonds. 18K yellow, pink, and white gold. 1960s.

*Courtesy of Antiquorum Auctioneers*

(above) Piaget Polo. Rectangular, quartz. 18K yellow gold and onyx. 1990s.
*Courtesy of Antiquorum Auctioneers*

(below) Piaget Hexagon. Yellow gold and diamonds. Agate bezel. 1970s.
*Courtesy of Antiquorum Auctioneers*

# PIAGET

(left) Piaget Possession. 18K white gold and diamonds. Quartz.
*Courtesy of Antiquorum Auctioneers*

(right) Piaget. White gold and diamonds, textured bracelet. 1960s.
*Courtesy of Antiquorum Auctioneers*

(left) Piaget. 18K white gold, onyx and diamonds. 1990s.
*Courtesy of Antiquorum Auctioneers*

(below) Piaget. White gold, diamond-set mother-of-pearl dial. 1970s.

*Courtesy of Antiquorum Auctioneers*

(above) Piaget Dual Time Zone. Horizontal oval, white gold. 1970s.

*Courtesy of Antiquorum Auctioneers*

(above) Piaget. 18K white gold, turquoise, and diamonds. 1990s.

*Courtesy of Antiquorum Auctioneers*

(right) Piaget ultra-thin quartz. Yellow gold and mother-of-pearl. 1980s.

*Courtesy of Antiquorum Auctioneers*

(top) Piaget Limelight.
Round, mechanical. White
gold and diamonds.
Current.
*Piaget*

(above) Piaget Emperador.
Cushion-shaped, perpetual
calendar, self-winding.
White gold and diamonds.
Current.
*Piaget*

(below) Piaget 18K yellow gold and
agate bracelet watch. Circa 1980.
*Courtesy of Antiquorum Auctioneers*

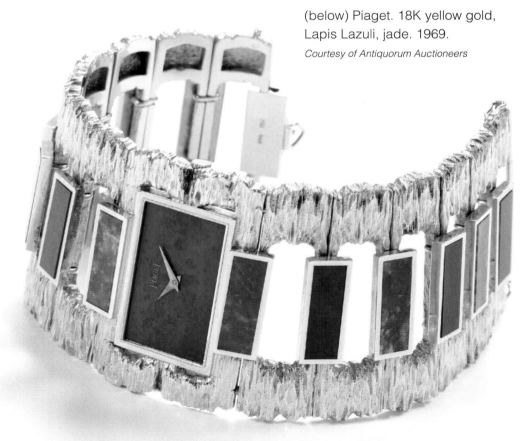

(below) Piaget. 18K yellow gold,
Lapis Lazuli, jade. 1969.
*Courtesy of Antiquorum Auctioneers*

(below) Piaget Titanium Grande Polo. Titanium and steel, 2010.

*Courtesy of Antiquorum Auctioneers*

(above) Piaget. 18K yellow gold, rubies, emeralds, and diamonds. Quartz. Circa 2000.

*Courtesy of Antiquorum Auctioneers*

(left) Piaget malachite dial.
Large, chain-link bracelet.
18K yellow gold. 1970s.
*Courtesy of Antiquorum Auctioneers*

(below) Piaget Altiplano
skeleton. Black PVD-coated
white gold. 2011.

(below) Piaget Tanagra. 18K yellow gold, diamonds, and rubies. Quartz, circa 2000.

*Courtesy of Antiquorum Auctioneers*

(above) Piaget Emperador. Chronograph, registers, automatic. 18K yellow gold. Circa 2008.

*Courtesy of Antiquorum Auctioneers*

(below) Piaget Chronometre 200M Automatique. 18K white and yellow gold. 2000s.

*Courtesy of Antiquorum Auctioneers*

(above) Piaget Miss Protocole. Rectangular, yellow gold and diamonds. 2007.

*Courtesy of Antiquorum Auctioneers*

(above) Piaget. Rectangular, 18K and diamonds, pave-set diamond dial. Circa 2000.

*Courtesy of Antiquorum Auctioneers*

(below) Piaget Polo Key Largo automatic. 18K white gold and diamonds. 1990s.

*Courtesy of Antiquorum Auctioneers*

(left) Piaget. White gold, diamonds, and rubies. Mother-of-pearl dial. 2000s.

*Courtesy of Antiquorum Auctioneers*

# Record Watch Company

Record was founded in 1903. The company was located in Tamelan in Switzerland's Jura region. Record merged with several other watch making companies in 1916. The new company styled itself the Record Dreadnought Watch Company, but reverted to the Record Watch Company in 1949. Record introduced their automatic hammer movement in 1944 and their rotor automatic in 1952. In 1960, Record launched the Caliber 435B pocket watch which was to become widely used on the American railroads.

Longines acquired Record in 1961 but the brand remained technically independent. Some Record models were marketed as Longines watches to attract higher prices. Record was closed down in 1991, another victim to the quartz crisis. Longines is now part of the Swatch group.

(below) Record. 9K gold. Manual wind, subsidiary seconds. 1950.

*littlecogs.com*

(right) Record chronograph, registers. Stainless steel. 1960s.

*Courtesy of Antiquorum Auctioneers*

(above and below) Record 18K yellow gold. Claw lugs. 1940s.
*Courtesy of Antiquorum Auctioneers*

(left) Record. Stainless steel, manual wind, screw back. Vintage.

*littlecogs.com*

(right) Record
chronograph.
Stainless steel and
pink gold. 1940s.
*Courtesy of Antiquorum
Auctioneers*

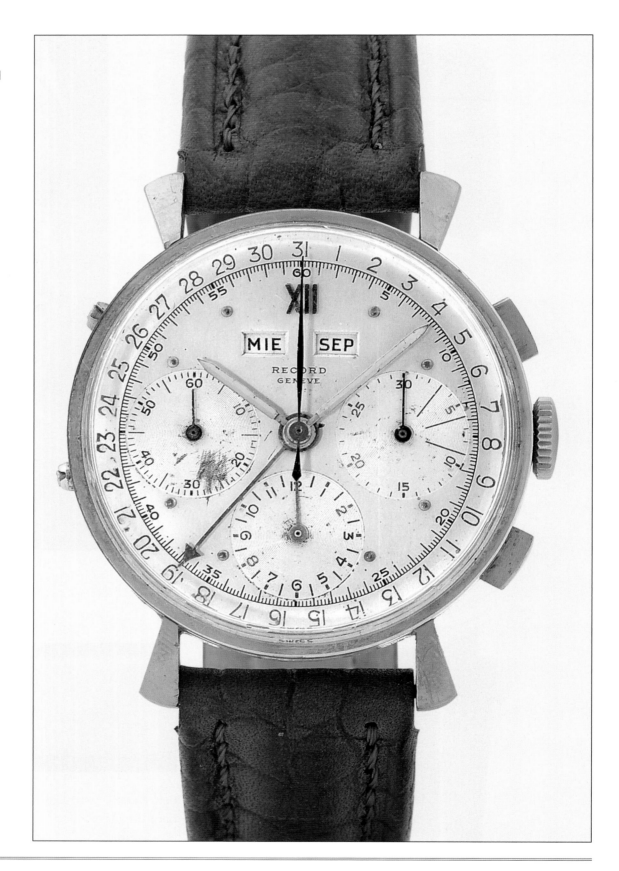

(left) Record. Rectangular, subsidiary seconds. 1960s.

*littlecogs.com*

(below) Record triple calendar, moon phases. Pink gold-plated. Vintage.

*Trebor's Vintage Watches*

# *Rolex*

Rolex was founded in 1905 by German émigré Hans Wilsdorf in London, England's Hatton Garden jewelry district. The company was originally called Wilsdorf and Davis. This was the era of pocket watches, but Wilsdorf was always interested in developing a technically perfect wristwatch. His first timepieces used Aegler movements. Wilsdorf registered the Rolex trademark in 1908, and had developed his own movement by 1910, which was endorsed by the Swiss School of Horology. In 1914 London's Kew Observatory certified Wilsdorf's timepiece with a Class A precision certificate, which meant that it was as accurate as a marine chronometer. This was a tremendous achievement at a time when wristwatches were notoriously unreliable. In 1919, Wilsdorf moved the company to La Chaux-de-Fonds, Switzerland. His move was driven by purely pragmatic reasons, including the heavy taxes levied by England on luxury imports and on the gold and silver Wilsdorf needed to make his watches.

Once Rolex had manufactured an accurate watch, the next step was to make it waterproof. This was achieved in 1926 by the invention of a new screw-top crown and casebook, which prevented water from seeping into the movement. Wilsdorf named the watch the "Oyster." Rolex demonstrated the properties of the watch by submerging their timepieces in water-filled shop displays. Wilsdorf promoted the watch by giving a gold-cased Oyster to the famous swimmer Mercedes Gleitze as she swam across the English Channel in 1927. Wilsdorf advertized the Oyster as the "Wonder Watch that Defies the Elements."

A series of iconic Rolex models followed the Oyster. The first self-winding wristwatch, the Perpetual Rotor was launched by the company in 1931. The movement of the wearer's arm kept this revolutionary timepiece fully wound. The watch soon became prestigious and sought-after. In World War II, the Oyster Perpetual became the timepiece of choice for British Royal Air Force pilots. During the War, Wilsdorf also supplied over three-thousand replacement watches to British prisoners of war in Germany whose Rolexes had been confiscateby the German camp guards. The recipients included Corporal Clive James Nutting, one of the organizers of the Great Escape from Stalag Luft III. The watch was delivered to him at the camp on July 10, 1943.

After the War, Rolex introduced a further spate of historic models. The Datejust in 1945, the Explorer, Turn-O-Graph, and Submariner appeared in 1953, followed by the GMT-Master in 1955 and the magnetically resistant Millgauss model in 1956. During the 1950s, Rolex developed a series of professional models aimed at deep-sea divers, aviators, mountain climbers, and scientific explorers. It is said that Sir Edmund Hillary wore a Rolex Oyster Perpetual when he climbed Everest in 1953. A revised Submariner was launched in 1959. The Cosmograph Daytona was launched in 1963, followed by the Sea-Dweller Submariner and the Date Feature Submariner in 1966. The orange-handed Explorer model appeared in 1971. Following the lead of the Japanese watch manufacturers, Rolex also developed quartz movement watches, including the Oysterquartz in 1973.

Hans Wilsdorf died in 1960 and was replaced as the head of Rolex by Andre Heiniger in 1962. The company is owned by a private trust and its shares are not traded. Rolex has retained its technical mastery and has continued to add classic models to its range, including the Yacht-Master sport watch in 1992. One of the company's newest innovations is the ceramic bezel. Rolex currently produces around 650,000 watches a year in its manufacturing facilities, which include its factory at Biel, Switzerland. In total, Rolex has four-thousand watchmakers employed in over a hundred countries. The company headquarters are in Geneva, Switzerland.

Rolex is one of the hundred most valuable brands in the world, and the leading name in luxury wristwatches. The company's watches are endorsed by many great artists and sportsmen. Rolex has also been the official timekeeper at Wimbledon since 1978, and at the 24 heures du Mans motor race.

(above and below) Rolex yellow gold
Air-King, Explorer dial, center
seconds, 1955.

*Image courtesy of Antiquorum Auctioneers*

(above) Rolex watch with
silver case, circa 1916.
Manual wind, subsidiary
seconds, enamel dial,
hinged back.

*littlecogs.com*

(above) Rolex gold shell
over stainless steel Oyster
Perpetual Air-King, early
1950s.

*Image courtesy of Antiquorum
Auctioneers*

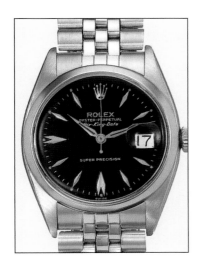

(left) Rolex Oyster Perpetual Air-King-Date, 1950s. Blue dial and stainless steel bracelet.

*Image courtesy of Antiquorum Auctioneers*

(left) Rolex Air-King, 1959. Black dial and leather strap.

*Image courtesy of Antiquorum Auctioneers*

(right) Rolex limited edition Air-King Cotton Bowl watch, 1967. Stainless steel and yellow gold. *Image courtesy of Antiquorum Auctioneers*

(below left) Rolex Air-King white dial, 2003.

*Trebor's Vintage Watches*

(below right) Rolex Air-King, yellow gold.

*littlecogs.com*

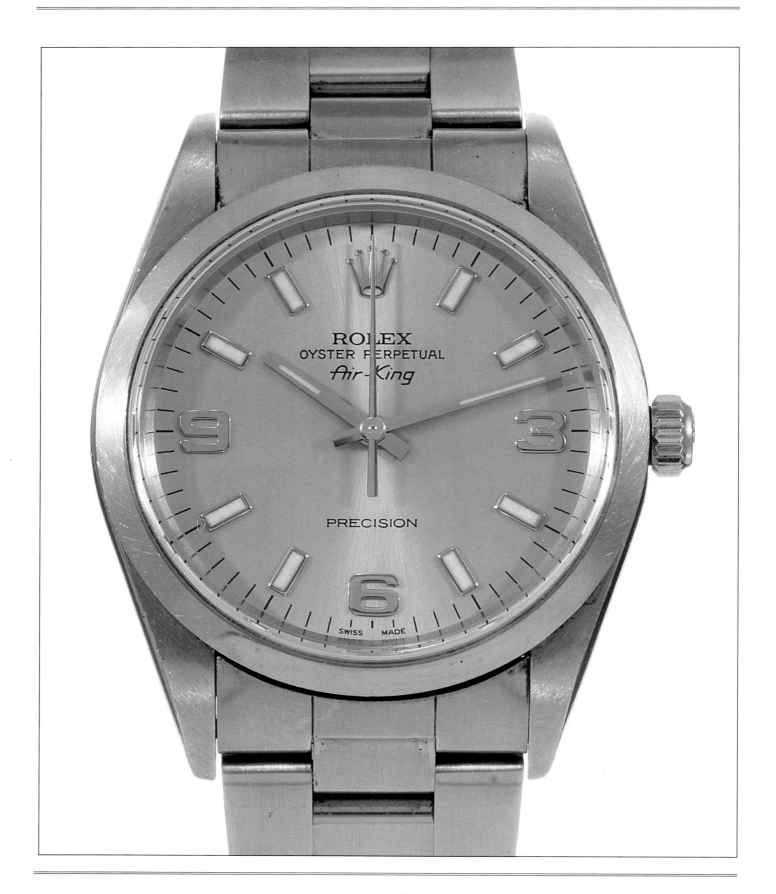

(left) Rolex stainless steel Air-King with pink face, 2002.

*Image courtesy of Antiquorum Auctioneers*

(below) Rolex. Stainless steel. Baton indexes. Subsidiary seconds. Vintage.

*littlecogs.com*

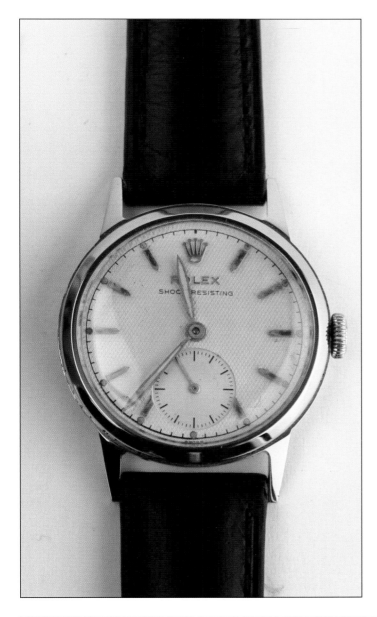

(above) Rolex Oyster Royal. Stainless steel. Shock resistant. Center seconds. Vintage.

*littlecogs.com*

(above) Rolex 18K yellow gold Roulette Datejust, 1956. Oyster Perpetual, crystal with Cyclops lens.

*Image courtesy of Antiquorum Auctioneers*

(above and left) Rolex Perpetual, stainless steel, center seconds, screw back, automatic superlative chronometer, circa 1968.

*littlecogs.com*

(below) Rolex Oyster Perpetual Datejust with moon phases, 1998. Stainless steel and enamel.
*Image courtesy of Antiquorum Auctioneers*

(bottom) Rolex Oyster Perpetual Air-King-Date, 18K yellow gold and stainless steel, 1970s.
*Image courtesy of Antiquorum Auctioneers*

(above) Rolex 18K yellow gold Oyster Perpetual, Datejust Thunderbird, 1962.
*Image courtesy of Antiquorum Auctioneers*

(above) Rolex Oysterdate, stainless steel,
center seconds with date, screw back and
crown, waterproof.
Circa 1980s.

*littlecogs.com*

(below) Rolex Turn-O-Graph, 2006. 18K pink gold with
red date. Stainless steel and 18K pink gold bracelet.

*Image courtesy of Antiquorum Auctioneers*

(right) Rolex Precision, stainless steel, manual wind, center seconds, circa 1980.

*littlecogs.com*

(above) Rolex Lady's Datejust, 18K yellow gold with diamond-set bezel, 1993.

*Image courtesy of Antiquorum Auctioneers*

(right) Rolex Lady's Datejust, platinum with diamond-set bezel, 2000.

*Image courtesy of Antiquorum Auctioneers*

(above) Rolex Oyster Perpetual, circa 1980s. Stainless steel, center seconds with date. Case number 15000.
*littlecogs.com*

(left) Rolex Datejust, 1980s. 18K yellow gold, diamond, and sapphire lady's watch, Pearlmaster bracelet.
*Image courtesy of Antiquorum Auctioneers*

(right) Rolex Datejust Pearlmaster, 2000. White gold, diamond-set bezel, diamond indexes.
*Image courtesy of Antiquorum Auctioneers*

(right) Rolex Oyster
Perpetual Datejust,
black dial.

*littlecogs.com*

(far right) Rolex
Datejust, circa
1990s.

*littlecogs.com*

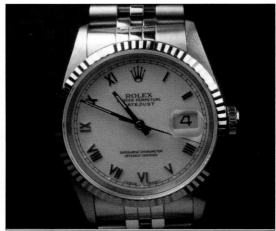

(right) Rolex Oyster
Perpetual Datejust
steel and gold, 1980.

*Trebor's Vintage Watches*

(above) Rolex Paul Newman, Oyster Cosmograph Daytona,
stainless steel, 1968. Anti-reflective black tachometer bezel.

*Image courtesy of Antiquorum Auctioneers*

(right) Rolex Paul Newman
Black Oyster Mark II dial,
Cosmograph Oyster Daytona
case. Stainless steel, black
bezel, 1971.

*Image courtesy of Antiquorum*

*Auctioneers*

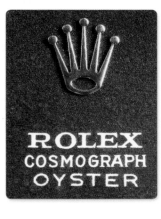

(below) Rolex Cosmograph Daytona Paul Newman.
14K yellow gold with round button chronograph, 1967.

*Image courtesy of Antiquorum Auctioneers*

(below) Rolex Oyster Perpetual Day-Date, 1982. White gold, diamond indexes. Center seconds, self-winding, water-resistant. Black leather strap and Rolex buckle.

*Image courtesy of Antiquorum Auctioneers*

(above) Rolex Day-Date, circa 1972. Pink gold case and bracelet. Diamond indexes with luminous pink gold baton hands.

*Image courtesy of Antiquorum Auctioneers*

(right) Rolex Oyster Perpetual Day-Date, circa 1959. 18K white gold with black leather strap.

*Image courtesy of Antiquorum Auctioneers*

(below) Rolex Oyster Perpetual Day-Date, 2001. 18K white gold and diamond. Center seconds, water-resistant, double quick-set day and date.

*Image courtesy of Antiquorum Auctioneers*

(left) Rolex Day-Date with green enamel dial. 18K yellow gold case, 1972.
*Image courtesy of Antiquorum Auctioneers*

(below) Rolex Oyster perpetual Day-Date with unusual birch dial. 18K yellow gold case, circa 1978.
*Image courtesy of Antiquorum Auctioneers*

(above) Rolex Oyster Perpetual Explorer II, 2000. Orange luminous black skeleton hands and leather strap. Two time zone, center seconds, stainless steel.

*Image courtesy of Antiquorum Auctioneers*

(right) Rolex Oyster Perpetual Explorer, 1958. Shock-resistant, water-resistant, self-winding, 1958.

*Image courtesy of Antiquorum Auctioneers*

(below) Rolex Oyster Perpetual Pre-Explorer with linen dial, 1953. Center seconds, self-winding, water-resistant, stainless steel.
*Image courtesy of Antiquorum Auctioneers*

(above) Rolex Explorer II, Oyster Perpetual, black spider dial, self-winding, 24-hour bezel, 1986.
*Image courtesy of Antiquorum Auctioneers*

(right) Rolex Oyster Perpetual Explorer with gilt dial, 1972. Stainless steel watch with luminous Arabic numerals and baton indexes.
*Image courtesy of Antiquorum Auctioneers*

(right) Rolex Steve McQueen Explorer II, 1976. 24-hour bezel, large orange arrow hand, stainless steel.

*Image courtesy of Antiquorum Auctioneers*

(left) Rolex GMT Master, automatic center seconds, screw back with date. Circa 1985.

*littlecogs.com*

(left) Rolex GMT Master II, 1991. Diamond and ruby dial, stainless steel and 18K yellow gold, 24-hour bezel.
*Image courtesy of Antiquorum Auctioneers*

(right) Rolex GMT Master, 1968. Stainless steel watch with chocolate dial, red and blue revolving bezel.
*Image courtesy of Antiquorum Auctioneers*

(leftt) Rolex Oyster Perpetual GMT Master, 1984. 18K yellow gold, bronze dial, bronze 24-hour bezel, and Rolex Jubilee bracelet.
*Image courtesy of Antiquorum Auctioneers*

Rolex Oyster Perpetual Milgauss, 2007. Anti-magnetic shield, stainless steel. White dial with orange baton indexes.

*Image courtesy of Antiquorum Auctioneers*

(above) Rolex Oyster Perpetual Milgauss, 1969. Anti-magnetic, water-resistant, stainless steel, Rolex Oyster bracelet.

*Image courtesy of Antiquorum Auctioneers*

(left) Rolex Datejust, stainless steel , center seconds, automatic. Rolex polo prize 1993, a rare presentation piece.

*littlecogs.com*

(above) Rolex Oyster Perpetual Green Milgauss, 2007. Stainless steel with green sapphire crystal, anti-magnetic shield. Orange-colored indexes and five-minute markers.

*Image courtesy of Antiquorum Auctioneers*

(above) Rolex Milgauss Bamford, stainless steel with PVD coating, 2007. Luminous white gold baton hands and blue lightning seconds hand.
*Image courtesy of Antiquorum Auctioneers*

(right) Rolex Datejust Oysterquartz, 1997. Stainless steel with matte silver dial.
*Image courtesy of Antiquorum Auctioneers*

(below) Rolex steel and 14K yellow gold Oysterquartz Datejust, 1979. Center seconds, water-resistant.

*Image courtesy of Antiquorum Auctioneers*

(above left) Rolex Precision, gold with cord bracelet, circa 1930s.

*Trebor's Vintage Watches*

(above right) Rolex Oyster Perpetual Turn-O-Graph, 1980. Dedication in Arabic.

*Image courtesy of Antiquorum Auctioneers*

(below) Rolex Precision, 9K gold, manual, center seconds, snap back. Hallmarked London, England 1960.

*littlecogs.com*

(left) Rolex manual wind, pink gold circa 1950s.

*Trebor's Vintage Watches*

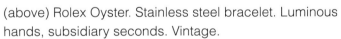

(above) Rolex Oyster. Stainless steel bracelet. Luminous hands, subsidiary seconds. Vintage.

*littlecogs.com*

(right) Rolex Oyster Perpetual. Stainless steel. Center seconds. Vintage.

*littlecogs.com*

(above and below) Rolex Oyster Precision, circa 1950. Stainless steel, manual wind, center seconds, serial number 692248, screw back.

*littlecogs.com*

(above) Rolex Oyster Royal, stainless steel, circa 1940s. Manual wind, center seconds, half hunter, screw back.

*littlecogs.com*

(below) Rolex Oyster automatic bubbleback, circa 1940s.

*Trebor's Vintage Watches*

(above) Rolex Oyster Perpetual Date. Stainless steel. Vintage.

*littlecogs.com*

(rigth) Rolex Oyster Perpetual Submariner diver's wristwatch, spider dial, 1988.

*Image courtesy of Antiquorum Auctioneers*

(below) Rolex Oyster Perpetual Datejust Submariner, 1980. Yellow gold with black dial and black bezel with compression times.

*Image courtesy of Antiquorum Auctioneers*

(below) Rolex Submariner, 5517 Tribute, customized by Military. DLC-coated stainless steel, 1991. Luminous steel sword hands.

*Image courtesy of Antiquorum Auctioneers*

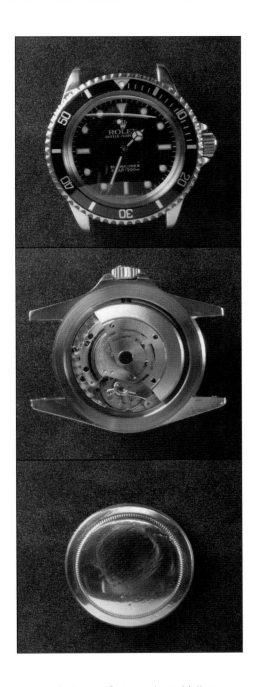

(above) Rolex Submariner. Yellow gold with black bezel.

*littlecogs.com*

(below) Rolex Submariner with Explorer dial, circa 1955. Stainless steel diver's watch with bi-directional revolving black bezel.

*Image courtesy of Antiquorum Auctioneers*

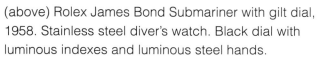

(above) Rolex James Bond Submariner with gilt dial, 1958. Stainless steel diver's watch. Black dial with luminous indexes and luminous steel hands.

*Image courtesy of Antiquorum Auctioneers*

(left) Rolex
Submariner, 1966

*Trebor's Vintage Watches*

(above) Rolex Submariner, tropical gilt dial,
1965. Stainless steel diver's watch.

*Image courtesy of Antiquorum Auctioneers*

(below) Rolex Pro-Hunter DeepSea Sea-Dweller, 2009. PVD-coated stainless steel diver's wristwatch with helium escape valve. Bezel with Cerachrom insert. Black dial with white gold indexes and luminous white gold skeleton hands.

*Image courtesy of Antiquorum Auctioneers*

(above) Rolex Submariner, 1981. 18K yellow gold case with blue bezel, black leather strap, and gold Rolex buckle. Color change dial with luminous gold indexes.

*Image courtesy of Antiquorum Auctioneers*

(left) Rolex Submariner retailed by Tiffany & Co., 1992. Stainless steel and 18K yellow fold diver's watch. Navy blue dial with luminous gold indexes and skeleton hands.
*Image courtesy of Antiquorum Auctioneers*

(below) Rolex Double Red Sea-Dweller II, 1975. Stainless steel diver's chronometer wristwatch with double red Sea-Dweller logo and helium escape valve. Black dial with luminous baton indexes.
*Image courtesy of Antiquorum Auctioneers*

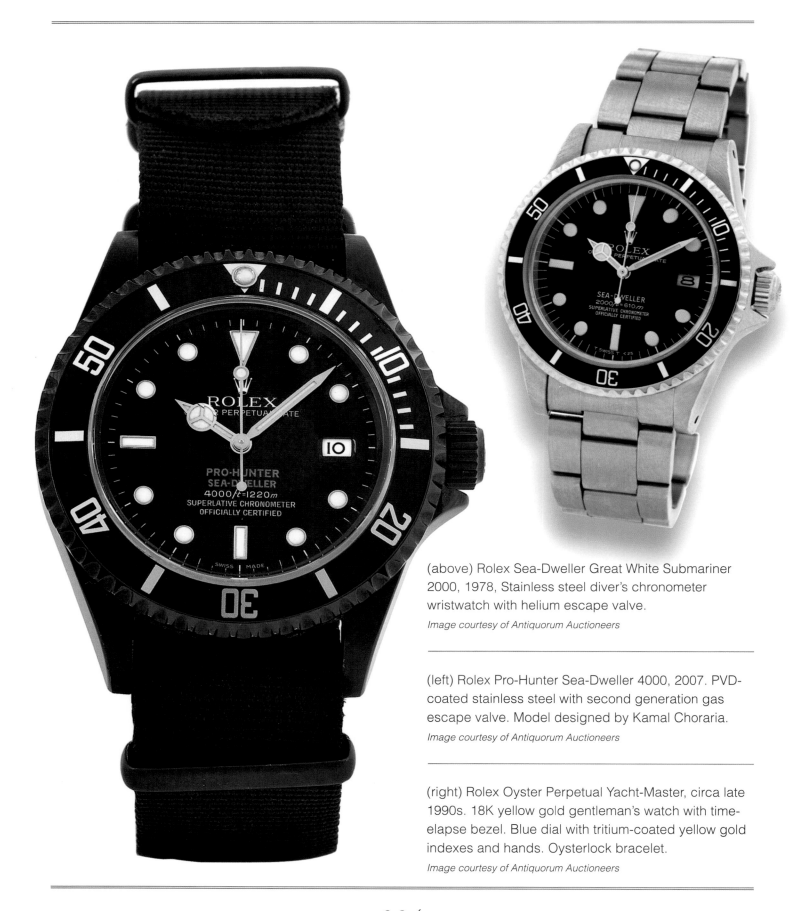

(above) Rolex Sea-Dweller Great White Submariner 2000, 1978, Stainless steel diver's chronometer wristwatch with helium escape valve.
*Image courtesy of Antiquorum Auctioneers*

(left) Rolex Pro-Hunter Sea-Dweller 4000, 2007. PVD-coated stainless steel with second generation gas escape valve. Model designed by Kamal Choraria.
*Image courtesy of Antiquorum Auctioneers*

(right) Rolex Oyster Perpetual Yacht-Master, circa late 1990s. 18K yellow gold gentleman's watch with time-elapse bezel. Blue dial with tritium-coated yellow gold indexes and hands. Oysterlock bracelet.
*Image courtesy of Antiquorum Auctioneers*

(right) Rolex Oyster
Perpetual Datejust Yacht-
Master 2007. Stainless
steel and platinum, with
bi-directional revolving
frosted bezel. Frosted
platinum dial and
sapphire crystal.
*Image courtesy of
Antiquorum Auctioneers*

(left) Rolex Yacht-Master, 2003. Stainless steel and platinum with platinum bezel. Water-resistant, self-winding, stainless steel Fliplock Oyster bracelet.
*Image courtesy of Antiquorum Auctioneers*

(below) Rolex Oyster Perpetual Datejust Yacht-Master, 2009. 18K yellow gold and stainless steel with time-lapse bezel. Sapphire crystal with Cyclops lens.
*Image courtesy of Antiquorum Auctioneers*

(left) Rolex Oyster Perpetual Datejust Yacht-Master, 1992. 18K yellow gold gentleman's watch with revolving bezel. White dial and Fliplock Oyster bracelet.
*Image courtesy of Antiquorum Auctioneers*

## The Rolex Cellini Collection

Named for the Renaissance master craftsman Benvenuto Cellini, Rolex's Cellini Collection consists of highly decorative and embellished wristwatches for both men and women. Some of the Cellini watches are rectangular in the style of the 1928 Cellini Prince model.

(above) Rolex Cellini, Genève, 2008. White gold, cushion-shaped case with concave lugs and rounded bezel. White gold dauphine hands.
*Image courtesy of Antiquorum Auctioneers*

(left) Rolex Cellini, Genève, circa 1988. 18K yellow gold watch with integral bracelet. The case is set with amethysts, and the bezel and fancy lugs with diamonds. Lapis lazuli dial and yellow gold hands.
*Image courtesy of Antiquorum Auctioneers*

(above) Rolex Cellini, Genève, circa late 1970s. 18K white gold ultra-thin case with leather strap and 18K white gold buckle. Blue soleil dial with white gold baton hands.
*Image courtesy of Antiquorum Auctioneers*

(above) Rolex Cellini, Genève,
circa 1980s. Lady's watch with
18K white gold woven bracelet
and diamond-set bezel. Blue gold
dial with white gold baton hands.
*Image courtesy of Antiquorum Auctioneers*

(right) Rolex Cellini Danaos, Genève,
1999. 18K white gold cushion-
shaped watch with leather strap and
Rolex buckle. White dial with printed
Arabic numerals.
*Image courtesy of Antiquorum Auctioneers*

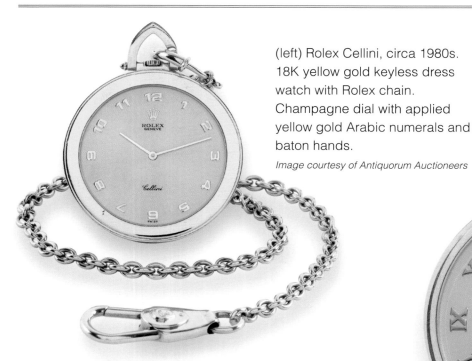

(left) Rolex Cellini, circa 1980s. 18K yellow gold keyless dress watch with Rolex chain. Champagne dial with applied yellow gold Arabic numerals and baton hands.
*Image courtesy of Antiquorum Auctioneers*

(below left) Rolex Cellini, circa 1970. Asymmetrical 18K white gold left-handed watch. Leather strap with plated Rolex buckle. Blue dial and white painted baton hands.
*Image courtesy of Antiquorum Auctioneers*

(below right) Rolex Cellini, Genève, 2006. White and pink gold cushion-shaped watch with pink gold bezel and concave lugs. Leather strap with white gold Rolex clasp.
*Image courtesy of Antiquorum Auctioneers*

(above) Rolex Cellini, Genève, early 2000s. 18K yellow gold with tubular link Rolex bracelet. Champagne dial with yellow gold baton hands.
*Image courtesy of Antiquorum Auctioneers*

(right) Rolex Cellini, Genève, 1991. 18K yellow gold with blue leather strap. Metallic blue dial with yellow gold dart indexes, yellow gold dauphine hands.
*Image courtesy of Antiquorum Auctioneers*

(above) Rolex Cellini Prince, 2006. Aerofoil shaped 18K yellow gold. Leather strap with double deployment clasp. Flat bezel with curved lugs. Two-tone champagne and white dial with yellow gold dauphine hands.

*Image courtesy of Antiquorum Auctioneers*

(left) Rolex Cellini, Genève, 2001. Platinum gentleman's watch with mother-of-pearl dial. Leather strap and platinum buckle.

*Image courtesy of Antiquorum Auctioneers*

(below) Rolex Cellini from the 1970s. White gold with integral Rolex bracelet. Silver dial with white gold indexes.

*Image courtesy of Antiquorum Auctioneers*

(above) Rolex Cellini diamond Orchid, 2001. White gold and lady's watch set with approximately eight carats of fine diamonds. Mother-of-pearl dial set with diamond indexes, white gold Alpha hands.

*Image courtesy of Antiquorum Auctioneers*

(right) Rolex Cellini Libertad, 1971. The watch commemorates the 1871 Treaty of Cordoba. 18K yellow gold with leather strap and Rolex buckle.

*Image courtesy of Antiquorum Auctioneers*

## Rolex Tudor

Hans Wilsdorf formed Rolex's Tudor division in 1946. Conceived as more affordable versions of the Rolex models, Tudor watches were constructed from less expensive materials and their movements were often bought-in from outside the company. Tudor cases were mostly made from stainless steel, and some were fitted with plastic glasses. Despite this, Tudor used several of the Rolex's model names, including Submariner and Chronograph. The brand has had some notable successes. Tudor Submariners were issued to United States Navy Seals, and divers in the French navy. Although Tiger Woods endorsed a series of colored-dial Tudor Rolexes in 1997, Tudor watches are not distributed in the United States.

(above) Rolex Tudor Prince Oysterdate Submariner Snowflake, 1968. Stainless steel diver's watch with bezel and blue dial.
*Image courtesy of Antiquorum Auctioneers*

(left) Rolex Tudor Automatic Chrono-Time, Genève, circa 1980s. Stainless steel self-winding, water-resistant with round button chronograph.
*Image courtesy of Antiquorum Auctioneers*

(above) Rolex Tudor, 9K yellow gold, manual wind, center seconds. 1964.

*littlecogs.com*

(above) Rolex Tudor Oysterdate Monte Carlo, 1970s. Stainless steel with chronograph, register, tachometer, and Rolex Oyster bracelet. Bicolor anthracite and black dial.

*Image courtesy of Antiquorum Auctioneers*

# *Rotary*

Moise Dreyfuss founded Rotary in 1895. His company was based in La Chaux-de-Fonds in the Swiss Jura. From the beginning Dreyfuss's prime objective was to offer good value. Rotary's motto is "Accuracy and distinction at a reasonable price." The company's famous winged wheel logo was adopted in 1925. Rotary was also innovative. It offered its first shockproof watch in 1934, its first automatic in 1942, and its first quartz model in 1973. Rotary was appointed the official watch supplier to the British army in 1940.

The company has continued to innovate in the twenty-first century. Rotary launched its Dolphin Marque in 2005. These watches can be worn for swimming and diving all day long. The diamond-set Rotary Rocks line was introduced in 2007, the Editions range appeared in 2008, and both the Aquaspeed and Les Originales lines were launched in 2009.

Rotary is still owned by the Dreyfuss family. Company chairman Robert Dreyfuss is the fourth generation to work in the business. The company headquarters are now in London, England but Rotary watches are still manufactured at the company's Swiss factory.

(below) Rotary Les Originales automatic. Stainless steel, black dial, rose gold indexes. Current.

*Rotary*

(above) Rotary manual wind. 9K gold. Center seconds, snap back. 1961.

*littlecogs.com*

(right) Rotary Aquaspeed chronometer. Stainless steel, rotating bezel. Current.
*Rotary*

(below) Rotary Aquaspeed chronometer. Stainless steel. Current.
*Rotary*

(above) Rotary ultra-slim, date. Gold-plated. Current model.
*Rotary*

(below) Rotary automatic. 9K gold, center seconds, date. 1972.
*littlecogs.com*

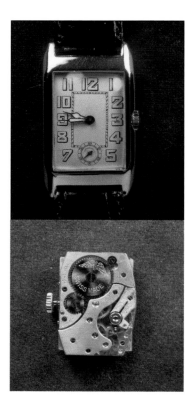

(right) Rotary manual wind. 9K gold. Subsidiary seconds, hinged back. Vintage.
*littlecogs.com*

(above) Rotary Evolution reversible chronograph. Multicolored dial. Current.
*Rotary*

# Seiko

Kintaro Hattori founded Seiko in 1881 in Tokyo, Japan. His company started by making wall clocks and pocket watches. Seiko launched Japan's first wristwatch, the Laurel in 1913. The company made Japan's first television commercial in 1953.

Seiko was technologically ambitious taking its inspiration from Hattori's maxim "Never look back, look forward, step forward." The company launched its iconic Grand Seiko watch in 1960 but its most important model the Seiko Quartz Astron followed in 1969. Although the first Astron was hugely expensive at 45,000 Yen, the watch started the quartz revolution in the watch-making industry. Seiko followed-up the Astron with the world's first LCD quartz watch in 1973 and the first multi-functional digital quartz watch in 1975. Several technology-inspired models followed. The first television watch and the first sound recorder watch were launched by Seiko in 1983 and the company launched the first computer watch in 1984. The Scubamaster computerized diver's watch followed in 1990. Seiko's Thermic watch, the world's first timepiece to be driven by body heat, was launched in 1998. The Ultimate Kinetic Chronograph and the Kinetic Automatic Relay followed in 1999 and the Kinetic Perpetual appeared in 2005. This was the world's first three-band radio watch. Seiko's Spectrum watch followed in 2006 with the first-ever electrophoresis display module. The company launched the Kinetic Direct Drive and Spring Drive Spacewalk models in 2007 and 2008.

Seiko has a reputation for outstanding accuracy and has been the official timekeeper at several Olympic Games.

(right) Seiko White Dolphin diver's watch. Ceramic and titanium, 2010.

*Courtesy of Antiquorum Auctioneers*

(left) Seiko World Time. Stainless steel, automatic. Center seconds, screw back. Vintage.

*littlecogs.com*

(below) Seiko Credor Egyptian. 18K yellow gold and diamond. Weave bracelet. 1990s.

*Courtesy of Antiquorum Auctioneers*

(left) Seiko Grand GS. Stainless steel, water-resistant. Center seconds, circa 2000.

*Courtesy of Antiquorum Auctioneers*

(left) Seiko Grand. Stainless steel. Chronometer, date. 1970s.

*Courtesy of Antiquorum Auctioneers*

(above) Seiko Grand. Water-resistant. Titanium. 2000.

*Courtesy of Antiquorum Auctioneers*

(left) Seiko automatic. Television-shaped, 18K yellow gold. Day/date. 1970s.

*Courtesy of Antiquorum Auctioneers*

# *Sekonda*

Sekonda is a British-based watchmaker. The company was set up in 1966 to distribute low-cost Russian-made watches. Russian-made Sekonda chronographs were worn by several Soyuz cosmonauts in the 1970s. After the quartz revolution, Sekonda began to manufacture in Hong Kong and its watches became more stylish and desirable. Sekonda has recently launched several new watch lines specifically aimed at younger customers. Seksy appeared in 2004, followed by One, Partytime, and Xpose. Sekonda's ethos is to offer excellent reliability at a competitive price. The company has been the best-selling watch brand in Great Britain for over twenty years.

(left) Sekonda. Small, ivory face. Spandex bracelet. Vintage.

*littlecogs.com*

(below) Sekonda. Cushion-shaped, roman numerals. Vintage.

*littlecogs.com*

(above) Sekonda. Stainless steel, square button chronograph. Register, telemeter, tachometer. Russian-made, 1950s.

*Courtesy of Antiquorum Auctioneers*

(above) Sekonda. Center seconds. Stainless steel back. Vintage.

*littlecogs.com*

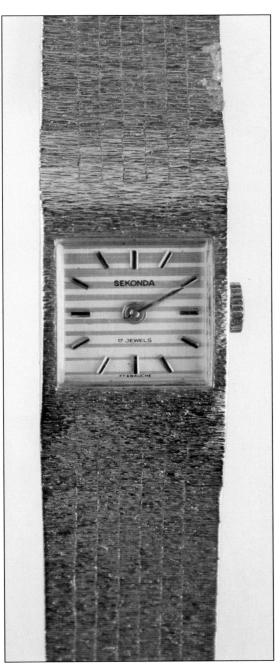

(above) Sekonda. Gold-plated, textured bracelet. Stainless steel back. Vintage.

*littlecogs.com*

(left) Sekonda. Stainless steel back. Date, center seconds. Vintage.

*littlecogs.com*

# Smiths

Samuel Smith established his watch-making company in London, England in 1851. The company received its first Royal warrant in 1907. Smiths became well-known for supplying aviation clocks and military stopwatches and wristwatches to the British Army. Smith watches were notoriously rugged, and were worn by members of the 1953 Everest Expedition. After the war, Smiths produced several wristwatch ranges for civilian customers including the De Luxe, Imperial, Astral, Everest, and Antarctic. The company also continued to make military timepieces and produced a general service watch for the Royal Air Force. Smiths ceased watch production in 1971. By this time, the company had diversified into several other areas of production including avionics.

(below and below right) Smiths W10. Stainless steel, black dial. Center seconds. 1969.

(above) Smiths chrome-plated De Luxe. Manual wind, subsidiary seconds. Vintage.

*littlecogs.com*

(below) Smiths De Luxe. Chrome-plated. Snap back. Vintage.

*littlecogs.com*

(above) Smiths Imperial. 9K gold. Center seconds, manual wind. 1960.

*littlecogs.com*

---

(right) Smiths Astral. Center seconds, manual wind. Vintage.

---

(below) Smiths 9K gold. Center seconds. 1960.

*littlecogs.com*

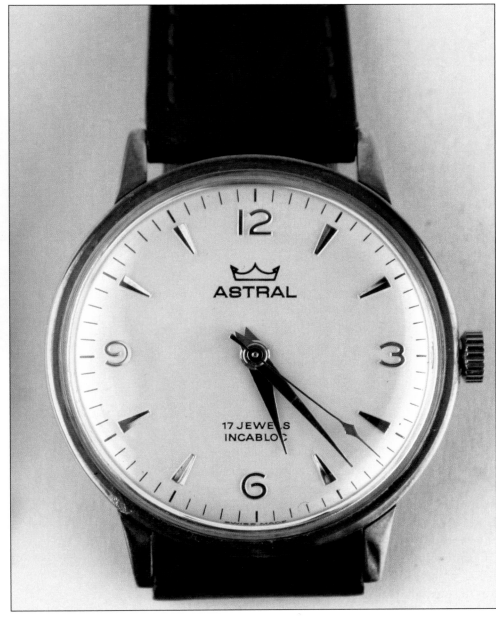

# *Swatch*

Swatch was born out of the quartz crisis of the 1970s, when the Swiss watch industry was being decimated by cheap imports from the Far East. The Swatch project was led by Franz Sprecher, a marketing consultant rather than a watchmaker. Swatch is a contraction of "second watch" and this is the central concept of the brand. Instead of having a single treasured timepiece, a Swatch customer can afford to build a collection of several different watches.

Swatch launched twelve versions of their iconic slim plastic watch in 1983. It was an instant success, and the watch soon became a cult classic. It is now the world's most successful watch of all time and has enabled Swatch to become the largest watch making business in the world. The Swatch Group now owns many prestige watch brands including Breguet, Omega, Longines, Tissot, and Mido. Its headquarters are at Biel in Switzerland, but the company has over one-hundred-and-fifty production centers around the world.

As well as producing plastic watches, Swatch now offers the Irony metal watch and the world's thinnest chronograph. Swatch also makes watches with unique technology. The Swatch Snowpass can be used as a ski pass at over seven-hundred ski resorts and the Swatch Beat features Swatch Internet Time.

Swatch sponsors several young sports, including BMX biking, surfing, and snowboarding. The company was the official timekeeper at the Snowboard World Cup.

New Swatch ranges include the Lacquered Collection, the Full-Blooded Collection, and the Chrono Collection. Early vintage Swatches are now highly collectible.

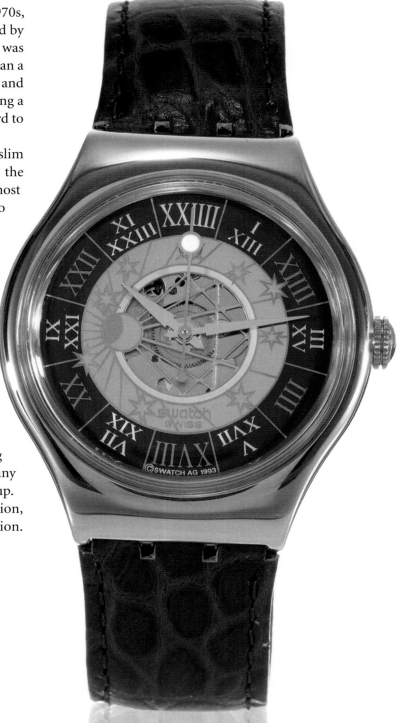

(right) Swatch Tresor Magique. Platinum. Tonneau-shaped. 1993.

*Courtesy of Antiquorum Auctioneers*

Swatch Charme de Crystal SKIN.
Color: Aurora Borealis. Circa 2005.
*Courtesy of Antiquorum Auctioneers*

Swatch Carousel Diaphane One.
Limited edition. Skeletonized.
2001.
*Courtesy of Antiquorum Auctioneers*

Swatch plastic quartz watch.
Center seconds. 1983.
*Courtesy of Antiquorum Auctioneers*

Swatch Kama Sutra.
Plastic quartz. 1993.
*Courtesy of Antiquorum
Auctioneers*

# Tiffany & Co.

Tiffany & Co. was founded in New York City in 1837 by partners Charles Lewis Tiffany and Teddy Young. The company soon became famous for its superlative jewelry, silverware, and watches. Its timepieces were manufactured at Tiffany's own Swiss factory, which became one of the largest watch manufacturing facilities in Switzerland. Founder's son Lewis Comfort Tiffany became the company's first design director in 1902 and the company has been at the forefront of American design from this time. Tiffanys has had many famous customers, including Abraham Lincoln and Lady Bird Johnson, and has also become a popular cultural icon. Tiffany and Co.'s flagship store was opened on New York City's Fifth Avenue in 1940.

The Tiffany Watch Company was founded in 2008. It is a collaborative venture between Tiffany & Co. and the Swatch Group. The Tiffany Watch Company makes both quartz and mechanical watches. These include the Gallery, Atlas, Gemea, Grand, and Tesoro ranges. Each Tiffany timepiece is sold with a five-year guarantee.

(above) Tiffany & Co. Power Reserve. 18K yellow gold. Forty-two-hour power reserve. Circa 2000.
*Courtesy of Antiquorum Auctioneers*

(left) Tiffany & Co. Regulator. 18K yellow gold. 2003.
*Courtesy of Antiquorum Auctioneers*

(above) Tiffany & Co. platinum and diamonds bracelet watch. 1920s.

*Courtesy of Antiquorum Auctioneers*

(right) Tiffany & Co. Digital Quartz. Rectangular, stainless steel. 1970s.

*Courtesy of Antiquorum Auctioneers*

(above) Tiffany & Co. Atlas. Automatic, chronometer, date. 18K yellow gold. Circa 2000.

*Courtesy of Antiquorum Auctioneers*

(left) Tiffany & Co. Tesoro quartz. Tonneau-shaped, 18K yellow gold. 1990s.

*Courtesy of Antiquorum Auctioneers*

(above) Tiffany & Co. platinum, stepped round bezel. Circa 2002.
*Courtesy of Antiquorum Auctioneers*

(right)Tiffany & Co. quartz. 18K yellow gold, diamond-set bezel. Circa 2000.
*Courtesy of Antiquorum Auctioneers*

# *Timex*

Timex was originally founded in Waterbury, Connecticut as the Waterbury Watch Company. It was one of many watchmakers located in Connecticut's Naugatuck Valley, an area known as the "Switzerland of America." Waterbury was one of the first watchmakers to use mass production techniques to produce cheap and reliable watches for the domestic market and export sales. By 1888, Waterbury had become the largest volume producer of watches in the world. In 1900, a Waterbury Yankee watch sold for just a dollar. In 1917, the company received a massive contract to supply watches to the United States army. Waterbury reached a license agreement with Walt Disney in 1930 and began to produce the famous Mickey Mouse watch. These became the company's first million dollar line. The Timex brand dates from 1957, when Waterbury launched their completely sealed watches. Although these watches couldn't be repaired, they were dustproof and rugged, and could "Take a licking and keep on ticking!" Timex was badly affected by the quartz revolution of the 1970s. Cheap imports flooded the market and the company was forced to cut its workforce from thirty thousand to six thousand. Timex re-focused on style and technological advances in the 1980s, and re-gained its commercial strength. Timex introduced the Ironman Triathlon watch in 1986, the Indiglo nightlight watch in 1992, and the Beepwear pager watch in 1998. Timex watches featuring satellite tracking, heart rate monitors, and lap timers are now available. In 1995, Fairchild Publications named Timex as America's favorite accessory brand. One out of every three watches sold in America is now made by Timex.

(below) Timex quartz. Water-resistant, stainless steel back. Vintage.

*littlecogs.com*

(above) Timex. Gold-plated, stainless steel back. Vintage.

*littlecogs.com*

# TIMEX

(left) Timex Rugged Analog. Resin case, Indiglo night light. Current.

*Timex*

(below) Timex classic dial. Water-resistant, center seconds, stainless steel back. Vintage.

*littlecogs.com*

(left) Timex Weekender. Water-resistant, degrade dial. Current.

*Timex*

(left) Timex Intelligent Quartz Altimeter. Indiglo night light. Current.

*Timex*

(below) Timex Intelligent Quartz Flyback Chronograph. Two time zone. Stainless steel, blue dial. Current.

*Timex*

(left)Timex brown dial. Water-resistant. Vintage.

littlecogs.com

(right) Timex stainless steel, integral bracelet. Water-resistant. Vintage.

*littlecogs.com*

(below) Timex gold-plated elliptical, brown dial. Stainless steel back. Vintage.

*littlecogs.com*

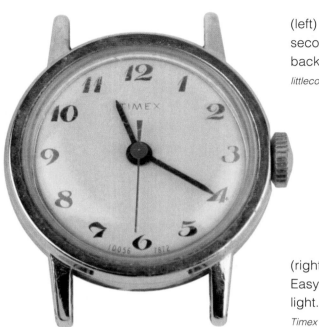

(left) Timex. Center seconds, stainless steel back. Vintage.

*littlecogs.com*

(right) Timex Originals Easy Reader. Indiglo night light. Current.

*Timex*

(below) Timex Originals 1950s. Inspired by classic Timex design. Current.

*Timex*

(left) Timex UK Time. Shock resistant, stainless steel. Vintage

*littlecogs.com*

# TIMEX

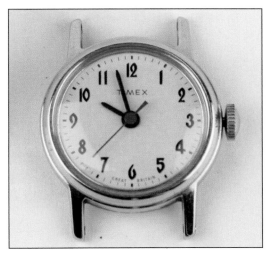

Timex stainless steel, center seconds. Vintage.

*littlecogs.com*

Timex heart-embossed bracelet. Center seconds, date. Vintage.

*littlecogs.com*

(left) Timex V-Conic escapement. Rectangular. Shock resistant. Vintage.

*littlecogs.com*

(below) Timex wide bezel, decorative lugs. Vintage.

*littlecogs.com*

(left) Timex. Ivory dial, water-resistant. Vintage.

*littlecogs.com*

Timex gold-plated oval face. Spandex bracelet. Vintage.

*littlecogs.com*

Timex Intelligent Quartz World Time. Stainless steel, water-resistant. Current.

*Timex*

Timex. Cushion-shaped, stainless back. Vintage.

*littlecogs.com*

(right) Timex. Rectangular, decorative lugs. Vintage.

*littlecogs.com*

(left) Timex oval dial, cushion-shaped bezel. Vintage.

*littlecogs.com*

(above) Timex Electric. Gold-plated, waterproof. Vintage.

*littlecogs.com*

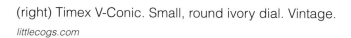

(right) Timex V-Conic. Small, round ivory dial. Vintage.

*littlecogs.com*

(left) Timex quartz digital, F cell. Stainless steel bracelet. Vintage.

*littlecogs.com*

(above) Timex quartz M cell. Center seconds. Vintage.

*littlecogs.com*

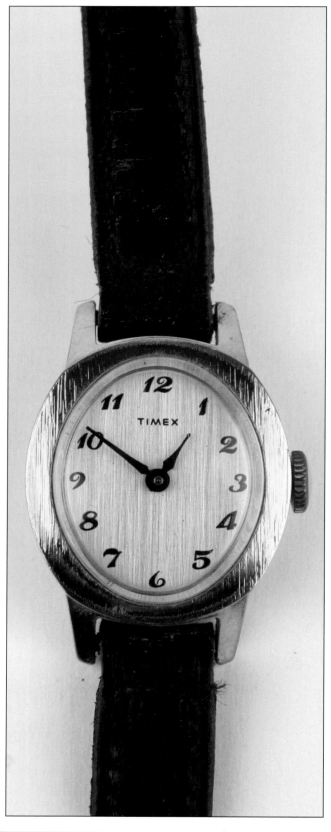

(right) Timex. Gold-plated, oval. Stainless steel back.
Vintage.

*littlecogs.com*

(left) Timex. Center seconds, water-resistant. Vintage.

*littlecogs.com*

(below) Timex. Baton indexes, stainless steel back. Vintage.

*littlecogs.com*

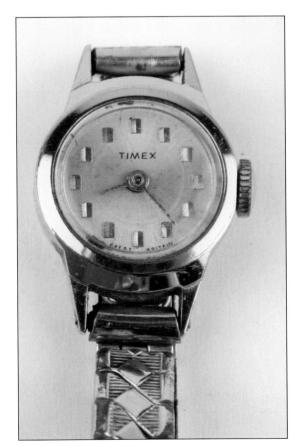

(above) Timex. Baton indexes. Date.

*littlecogs.com*

(above) Timex. Ivory dial, center seconds. Vintage.

*littlecogs.com*

(above) Timex. Early shockproof. Stainless steel back. Vintage.

*littlecogs.com*

(below) Timex. Stainless steel back, spandex bracelet. Vintage.

*littlecogs.com*

(left) Timex automatic. Water-resistant. Stainless steel. Vintage.

*littlecogs.com*

(below) Timex ivory dial, stainless steel back. Vintage.

*littlecogs.com*

(right) Timex quartz A cell. Day/date indicators. Vintage.

*littlecogs.com*

(below) Timex. TV-shaped. Day/date indicators. 1970s.

*littlecogs.com*

(left) Timex Ironman Race Trainer. Digital heart rate monitor pack. Current.

*Timex*

(right) Timex Ironman Tapscreen 150 Lap. Chronograph, lap counter. Current.

*Timex*

(right) Timex. Stainless steel, water-resistant. Center seconds. Vintage.

*littlecogs.com*

# Tissot

Tissot was founded in 1853 by Charles-Felicien Tissot and his son Charles-Emile Tissot in the Swiss Jura village of Le Locle. Self-styled "Innovator by tradition," Tissot was original and inventive from the beginning. The company has achieved many "firsts" in design, technology, and even in the use of materials. Tissot launched the Rock watch in 1985, the Pearl watch in 1987, and the Wood watch in 1988. The company developed the first antimagnetic watch in 1930, the first plastic mechanical watch in 1971, and the revolutionary T-Touch watch (with touch-screen technology) in 1999. Tissot has also launched a range of iconic watch models including the Navigator in 1953, the PR516 in 1965, the F1 in 1978, the Titanium 7 in 1998, the Silen-T in 2002, and the Sea-Touch in 2009.

Tissot watches have been worn by many famous people including Carmen Miranda, Grace Kelly, Elvis Presley, and Nelson Mandela. Today's Tissot Ambassadors include Danica Patrick the NASCAR and IndyCar race driver and Nicky Hayden the 2006 MotoGP World Champion.

Tissot is now owned by the Swatch Group.

(left) Tissot World Time. Self winding, center seconds. 18K pink gold. 1950s.
*Courtesy of Antiquorum Auctioneers*

(below) Tissot Touch Navigator. Stainless steel, quartz. Sapphire crystal. Current.

(below) Tissot T-Touch II. PVD-coated Titanium. Quartz. Current.

(above) Tissot World Time. Self-winding, water-resistant.
18K yellow gold. 1955.

*Courtesy of Antiquorum Auctioneers*

(right) Tissot quartz. Curved, rectangular. White,
diamond-patterned dial. Water-resistant. Current.

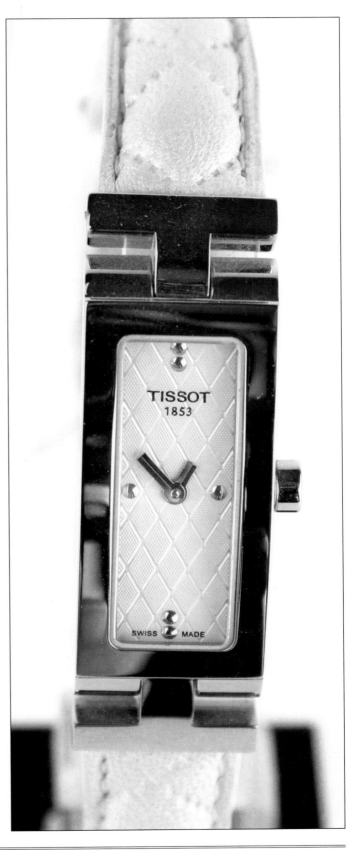

(left) Tissot Seastar.
Automatic, stainless
steel. Vintage.

*Trebor's Vintage Watches*

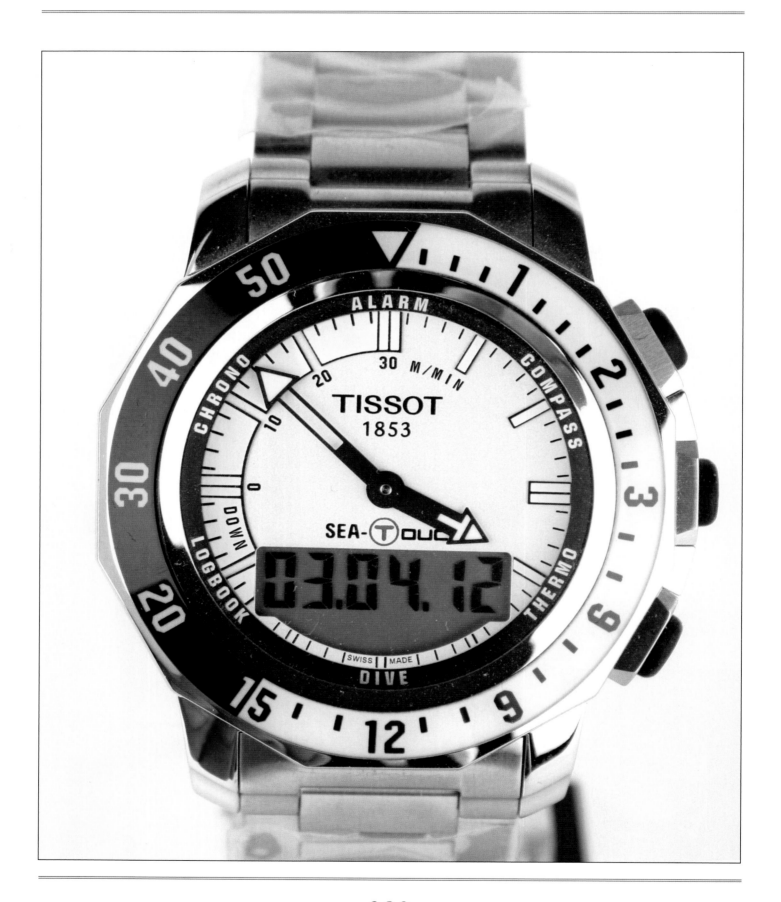

(left) Tissot chronograph. 18K yellow gold. Single olive button. 1940s.
*Courtesy of Antiquorum Auctioneers*

(below) Tissot World Time. Stainless steel, center seconds. 1950s.
*Courtesy of Antiquorum Auctioneers*

(below) Tissot PR516. PVD-coated steel. Quartz. Current.

(left) Tissot Sea-Touch large three-button chronometer. Digital, stainless steel. Alarm, compass. Current.

(left) Tissot Seamaster.
Manual wind. Yellow
gold-filled. 1970.

*Trebor's Vintage Watches*

(above) Tissot Tropical chronograph. 14K yellow gold.
1940s.

*Courtesy of Antiquorum Auctioneers*

(left) Tissot Steel Navigator chronograph. Register.
1950s.

*Courtesy of Antiquorum Auctioneers*

(above) Tissot Two
Americas. 14K yellow gold
cloisonné enamel dial.
1955.
*Courtesy of Antiquorum*
*Auctioneers*

(left) Tissot T-Lord. Automatic. Sapphire
crystal with anti-reflective coating. Current.

(right) Tissot 9K gold. Manual wind, center
seconds. 1961
littlecogs.com

(left) Tissot automatic chronometer, date. 18K pink gold. Circa 2000.
*Courtesy of Antiquorum Auctioneers*

(below) Tissot Stylist. Gold-plated, gold baton hands. 1960.
*Courtesy of Antiquorum Auctioneers*

(right) Tissot Seamaster. Manual wind. Yellow gold-filled. 1970.
*Trebor's Vintage Watches*

(above) Tissot chronograph. Staybrite stainless steel. 1945.
*Courtesy of Antiquorum Auctioneers*

(above) Tissot single button
chronograph. Staybrite stainless steel.
Register, tachometer. 1940s.
*Courtesy of Antiquorum Auctioneers*

(right) Tissot Veloci-T. Stainless steel.
Water-resistant, quartz. Current.

(above) Tissot Janeiro limited edition.
Stainless steel. Chronometer,
chronograph, date, tachymeter,
telemeter scales. 1996.
*Courtesy of Antiquorum Auctioneers*

(right) Tissot large chronograph.
Staybrite stainless steel, claw lugs.
1930s.
*Courtesy of Antiquorum Auctioneers*

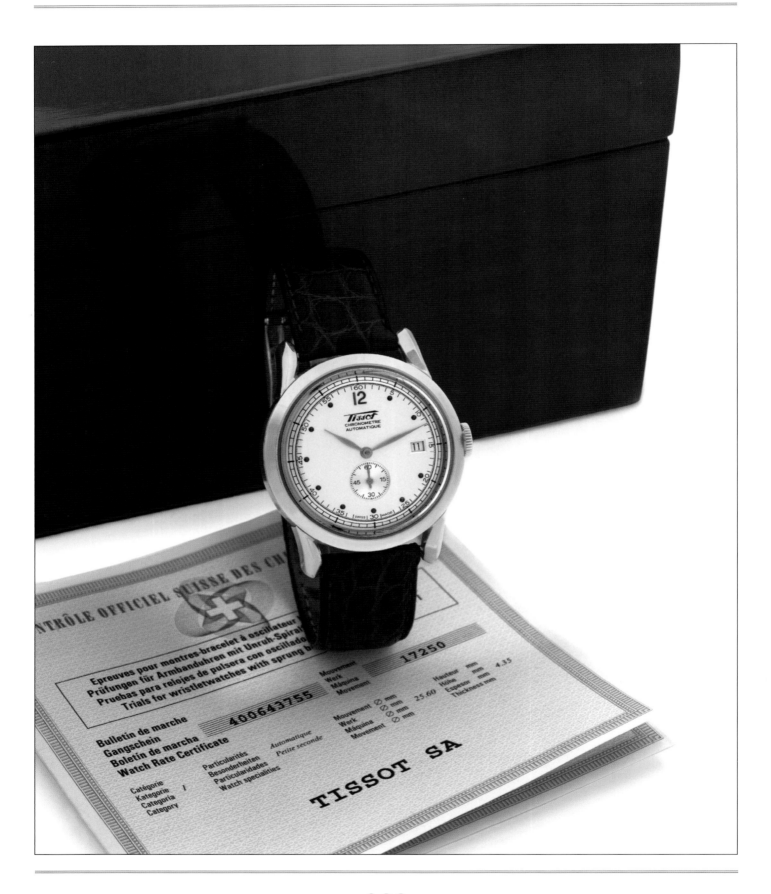

(left) Tissot Heritage. Three hand chronometer. 150th anniversary edition. 18K pink gold. 2003.

*Courtesy of Antiquorum Auctioneers*

(above) Tissot automatic. Stainless steel, center seconds. Screw back. Vintage.

*littlecogs.com*

(right) Tissot quartz. Stainless steel and ceramic. Round, white dial and bezel. Diamond markers. Current.

(left) Tissot 18K yellow gold, rectangular. Date. Current.

(below) Tissot Sailing-Touch. Stainless steel. Water-resistant, multi-functional. Current.

(above) Tissot T-Touch II. PVD-coated titanium, quartz. Current.

(above) Tissot Cabochon. Rectangular, stainless steel, cabochon sapphire. 1975.
*Courtesy of Antiquorum Auctioneers*

(below) Tissot Seamaster. PVD-coated steel. Automatic. Current.

Tissot quartz. Stainless steel, rectangular. Water-resistant, center seconds, date. Current.

(left) Tissot automatic. Stainless steel. Circa 1951.
*Trebor's Vintage Watches*

(right) Tissot Seastar. Automatic, date. TV-shaped. 1970s.
*Trebor's Vintage Watches*

(right) Tissot automatic. Stainless steel, sapphire crystal. Four-dial, three-button chronometer. Center seconds. Current.

(left) Tissot Seastar. Stainless steel, manual wind. Screw back. Vintage.

*littlecogs.com*

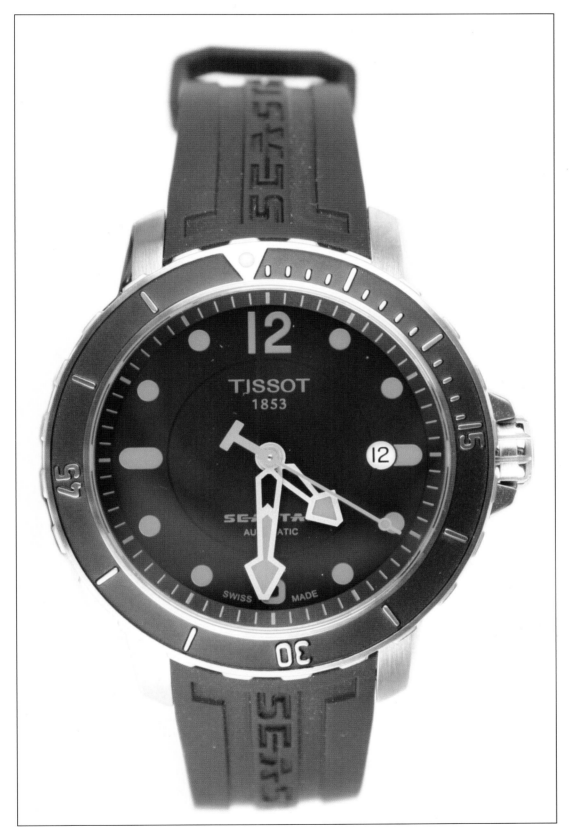

(above) Tissot
Antimagnetique.
Manual wind. Stainless
steel. 1940s.
*Trebor's Vintage Watches*

(left) Tissot Seastar
automatic. Oversized.
Orange hands and
markers. Black dial and
bezel. Center seconds.
Current.

# Ulysse Nardin

Watchmaker Ulysse Nardin learned his craft from his father, Leonard-Frederic Nardin. In 1846 he founded his watch making business in the Swiss village of Le Locle. Ulysse Nardin focused on manufacturing accurate and complicated chronometers. These timepieces were also highly decorated, and Nardin became famous for its fantastic enamelwork. In the twentieth century, the company became famous for its marine chronometers. Ulysse Nardin exported many watches to the Americas and South East Asia and the company name became known worldwide.

Ulysse Nardin was family-run until 1983 when the company was taken over by a group headed by Rolf W. Schnyder. The company launched several landmark astronomic chronometers in the 1980s. Many of these timepieces commemorated famous astronomers, including Galileo, Copernicus, and Kepler. The Ulysse Nardin Pulsometer and GMT Perpetual appeared in the 1990s.

Ulysse Nardin's distinctive anchor trademark is still associated with superlative decoration and precise mechanisms.

(left) Ulysse Nardin Lady Diver. Self-winding. Stainless steel and diamonds. Current.
*Ulysse Nardin*

(right) Ulysse Nardin Steel Split Chronograph Berlin 1907. Stainless steel. 1995.
*Courtesy of Antiquorum Auctioneers*

(above) Ulysse Nardin Black Sea.
Rubber-coated steel. Self-winding.
Current.

*Ulysse Nardin*

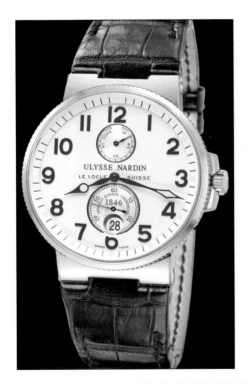

(above) Ulysse Nardin San Marco. Limited edition.
18K yellow gold. 2002.

*Courtesy of Antiquorum Auctioneers*

(left) Ulysse Nardin Maxi Marine Chronometer.
Stainless steel, leather strap. Current.

*Ulysse Nardin*

(above) Ulysse Nardin Anniversary 160. Self-winding. 18K white gold. Current.

*Ulysse Nardin*

(above) Ulysse Nardin Gorch Fock. Cloisonné enamel dial. 18K yellow gold. 1992.

*Courtesy of Antiquorum Auctioneers*

(right) Ulysse Nardin Michelangelo Gigante UTC Dual Time. Limited edition. 18K white gold, blue dial. Current.

*Ulysse Nardin*

(right) Ulysse Nardin Sonata Cathedral Dual Time. Large, two time zone. 18K white gold. 2006.

*Courtesy of Antiquorum Auctioneers*

(below) Ulysse Nardin Ludovico Perpetual Calendar. 18K yellow gold. Tonneau-shaped. Circa 2002.

*Courtesy of Antiquorum Auctioneers*

(below) Ulysse Nardin. 9K yellow gold. Manual wind, subsidiary seconds. 1948.

*littlecogs.com*

(below and right) Ulysse Nardin Twenty Dollar Coin watch. Coin dates from 1904. 18K yellow gold. 1960s.

*Courtesy of Antiquorum Auctioneers*

(right) Ulysse Nardin. Rectangular, fluted sides. 18K yellow gold. 1940s.

*Courtesy of Antiquorum Auctioneers*

(above) Ulysse Nardin Perpetual Calendar GMT. Curved, 18K white gold. 2005.

*Courtesy of Antiquorum Auctioneers*

(below) Ulysse Nardin Enamel Pulsations chronograph. 18K pink gold, enamel dial. 1940s.

*Courtesy of Antiquorum Auctioneers*

(above) Ulysse Nardin San Marco GMT. Two time zone. Stainless steel. 1996.

*Courtesy of Antiquorum Auctioneers*

(above) Ulysse Nardin chronograph. Cushion-shaped, 18K yellow gold. 1930s.

*Courtesy of Antiquorum Auctioneers*

(left) Ulysse Nardin GMT Big Date automatic. Time zone, permanent home time display. Vintage.

*littlecogs.com*

(above) Ulysse Nardin El Toro.
Limited edition. 18K red gold, black
ceramic bezel. Current.

*Ulysse Nardin*

(right) Ulysse Nardin Diavola for Only
Watch. Flying tourbillon regulator.
Stainless steel.

*Courtesy of Antiquorum Auctioneers*

(left) Ulysse Nardin The Freak Diamond Heart. Limited edition. Platinum and diamond. 2005.
*Courtesy of Antiquorum Auctioneers*

(right) Ulysse Nardin pink gold marine chronometer. Self-winding. Diver's watch. 2004.
*Courtesy of Antiquorum Auctioneers*

(right) Ulysse Nardin
Executive Dual Time.
Stainless steel, ceramic
bezel. Current.

*Ulysse Nardin*

(above) Ulysse Nardin Marine Chronometer. Diver's
watch. 18K yellow gold, midnight blue dial. 2003.

*Courtesy of Antiquorum Auctioneers*

(right) Ulysse Nardin Michelangelo Gigante
chronometer. Automatic. Tonneau-shaped, stainless
steel. Circa 2005.

*Courtesy of Antiquorum Auctioneers*

(left) Ulysse Nardin Marine Chronometer. Diver's watch. 18K pink gold case and bracelet sections. 2005.
*Courtesy of Antiquorum Auctioneers*

(below) Ulysse Nardin Maxi Marine Diver. Titanium chronometer. Luminous triangular indexes. 2010.
*Courtesy of Antiquorum Auctioneers*

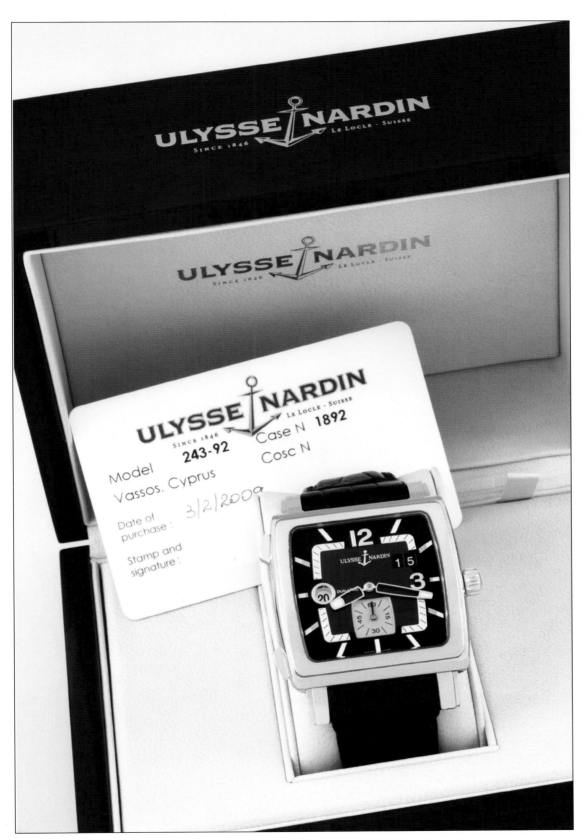

(left) Ulysse Nardin Steel Quadrato GMT. Two time zone. Curved, stainless steel. 2009.

*Courtesy of Antiquorum Auctioneers*

(below) Ulysse Nardin Red Marine Chronometer 1846. Stainless steel, titanium. Textured red and black dial. 2007.
*Courtesy of Antiquorum Auctioneers*

(above) Ulysse Nardin Perpetual Calendar GMT. 18K white gold. Self-winding, water-resistant. 1990s.
*Courtesy of Antiquorum Auctioneers*

(left) Ulysse Nardin Platinum Perpetual Calendar GMT Chronometer. Limited edition. Textured silver dial. 2003.
*Courtesy of Antiquorum Auctioneers*

(below) Ulysse Nardin Michelangelo Triple Calendar. Astronomic, moon phases. 18K yellow gold. 1980s.
*Courtesy of Antiquorum Auctioneers*

(above) Ulysse Nardin Circus Minute
Repeater. Aventurine dial, 18K white
gold. Current.

*Ulysse Nardin*

(above) Ulysse Nardin Tellurium Johannes Kepler. Astronomic, moon phases,
zodiac signs. 18K yellow gold, 1992.

*Courtesy of Antiquorum Auctioneers*

(left) Ulysse Nardin Forgerons Minute Repeater. Manual wind. 18K rose gold,
black onyx dial. Current.

*Ulysse Nardin*

(right) Ulysse Nardin San Marco Santa Catarina. 18K yellow gold, cloisonné
dial. 1995.

*Courtesy of Antiquorum Auctioneers*

(below) Ulysse Nardin chronograph. Cushion-shaped. 18K yellow gold. 1940.

*Courtesy of Antiquorum Auctioneers*

(above) Ulysse Nardin Ludovico Perpetual Calendar. Tonneau-shaped. 18K pink gold. 2002.

*Courtesy of Antiquorum Auctioneers*

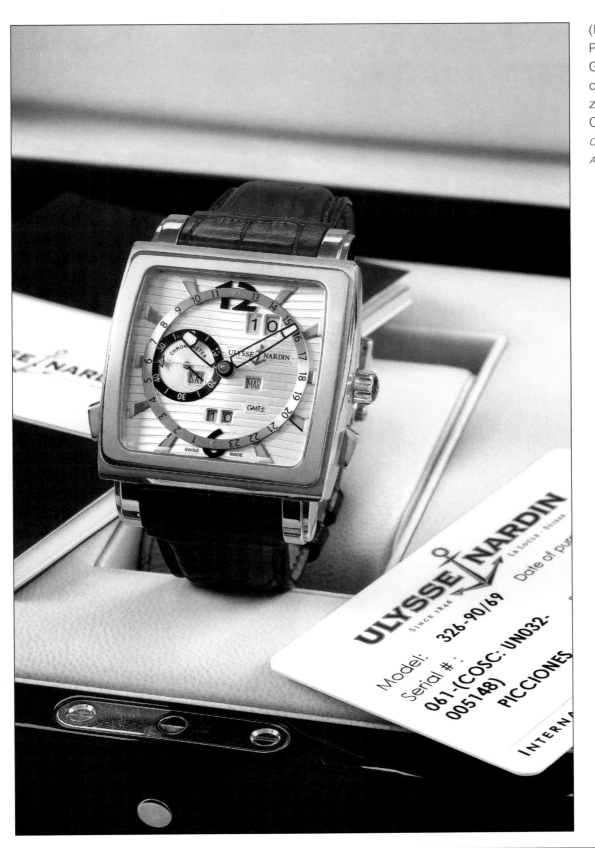

(left) Ulysse Nardin
Perpetual Calendar
GMT. Square,
curved, two time
zone. 18K pink gold.
Circa 2005.

*Courtesy of Antiquorum*
*Auctioneers*

# Universal Genève

Universal was founded by two partners in 1894. Watchmakers Numa-Emile Descombes and Ulysse Georges Perret were both from the Swiss town of Le Locle. Louis Edouard Berthoud joined the company in 1897. Universal created the Compur military wristwatch in 1933 and the Aero aviator's chronograph in 1936. These models helped the company to survive the Great Depression. Universal also supplied watches to the Dutch army until the country was invaded by the German army in 1939.

Universal launched several novel and inventive models after the war. These included the iconic Polerouter of 1954, the thinnest automatic of this era. The SAS used this watch on their polar missions. The Golden Shadow and White Shadow models were introduced in 1965, the Micorotor UG 66 in 1966, and the Unisonic Tuning watch in 1968.

Universal was taken over by Bulova in the late 1960s, and the two companies worked together to create electronic movements. The company launched several ultra-thin quartz watches in the 1970s, to compete with imports from the Far East.

Universal celebrated its hundredth anniversary with the reversible Janus in 1994. The company is now owned by Stelux Holdings but Universal's headquarters are still in Geneva, Switzerland.

Many famous people have worn Universal watches including Donald Trump, Joan Rivers, and President Harry S. Truman. Jean Cocteau was so impressed by his Universal that he designed a poster for the company.

(right) Universal Uni-Compax. Yellow gold, square-button chronograph. 1950s.

*Courtesy of Antiquorum Auctioneers*

(above) Universal rectangular. 18K yellow gold, textured mesh bracelet. 1970s.

*Courtesy of Antiquorum Auctioneers*

(above) Universal Railway. Porcelain white dial. Red sweep seconds. 1960s.

*Trebor's Vintage Watches*

(below) Universal manual wind. Stainless steel, snap back. Vintage.

*littlecogs.com*

(right) Universal. Integral mesh bracelet. 14K yellow gold. 1960s.

*Trebor's Vintage Watches*

(below) Universal 1986 Franklin Mint. Skeletonized, 18K yellow gold.

*Courtesy of Antiquorum Auctioneers*

(below) Universal Yard watch. Pink gold-topped. Manual wind. Vintage.

*littlecogs.com*

(above) Universal white gold and diamonds. Snake-link bracelet. 1960s.

*Courtesy of Antiquorum Auctioneers*

(right) Universal Compax chronograph. 18K yellow gold. Manual wind. Early 1950s.
*Trebor's Vintage Watches*

(above) Universal Compax. Stainless steel and yellow gold. Round-button chronograph. 2000.
*Courtesy of Antiquorum Auctioneers*

(above) Universal Aero-Compax chronograph. Large, two time zones. 1950s.
*Courtesy of Antiquorum Auctioneers*

(below) Universal Mono-poussoir. Silver case. Single coaxial button chronograph. 1920s.

*Courtesy of Antiquorum Auctioneers*

(above) Universal Jump Hour. Flared rectangle. 18K yellow gold. 1990s.

*Courtesy of Antiquorum Auctioneers*

(right) Universal Golden Janus Cabriolet. Reversible, double-dial. Platinum and 18K pink gold. 1994.

*Courtesy of Antiquorum Auctioneers*

(above) Universal Compax. Steel and 18K yellow gold.
Round-button chronograph. 2005.

*Courtesy of Antiquorum Auctioneers*

(right) Universal indirect center seconds. 18K yellow
gold. 1950s.

*Courtesy of Antiquorum Auctioneers*

(above) Universal Polerouter. 215 microtor automatic movement. Globe logo. Gold-filled. 1950s.

*Trebor's Vintage Watches*

((left) Universal Monodatic bumper model, date. 18K pink gold. 1950s.

*Courtesy of Antiquorum Auctioneers*

(below) Universal mechanical dress watch. Gold-filled, linen dial. 1960s.

*Trebor's Vintage Watches*

(right) Universal bumper automatic. Yellow gold-filled. Early 1950s.

*Trebor's Vintage Watches*

(far right) Universal Polerouter automatic. Date, microtor. 18K yellow gold. 1960s.

*Trebor's Vintage Watches*

(above) Universal South America. 18K rose gold, cloisonné enamel. 1946.

*Courtesy of Antiquorum Auctioneers*

(above) Universal tubular bangle wristwatch. 18K yellow gold. 1940s.

*Courtesy of Antiquorum Auctioneers*

(below) Universal skeletonized, thin. 18K yellow gold. 1990s.

*Courtesy of Antiquorum Auctioneers*

(above) Universal Golden Shadow. Large, ultra-slim, rectangular. 18K yellow gold. Circa 1963.

*Courtesy of Antiquorum Auctioneers*

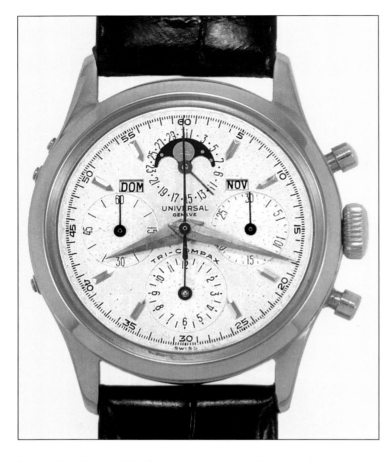

(above) Universal Tri-Compax. Astronomic, round-button chronograph. 18K pink gold. 1950.

*Courtesy of Antiquorum Auctioneers*

(below) Universal stainless steel, manual wind. Rectangular, baton indexes. Vintage.

*littlecogs.com*

(below) Universal Polerouter automatic. Large, stainless steel. 1960s.

*Courtesy of Antiquorum Auctioneers*

# *Uno*

Uno was originally founded in Switzerland by the three Dimier brothers in 1795. The company specialized in exporting watches to England and the Far East. The Uno brand name was sold to the Gaumont Watch Company of Manchester, England in the 1950s. Gaumont was a watch importer. Founded in 1939, the company became insolvent in 1998. Much later, famous watchmaker Klaus Botta revived the Uno trade name for his revolutionary one-hand watch. This iconic model was first launched in 1986.

(right) Uno watch. 9ct gold. Manual wind, subsidiary seconds. Two piece case. Hallmarked Birmingham 1951.
*littlecogs.com*

(below) Uno watch with enamel dial, Arabic hour markers. Subsidiary seconds. Silver case. Circa 1930s.

# Vacheron Constantin

Jean-Marc Vacheron founded his business in 1755 in Geneva, Switzerland. This means that Vacheron Constantin is one of the oldest watch making businesses in the world to have been in continual operation since its foundation. Francois Constantin joined the business in 1819. It was Constantin that coined the company motto "Do better if possible and that is always possible." Throughout its history Vacheron Constantin has always been committed to both technical and aesthetic excellence. The company's craftsmen are not only watchmakers, but master enamellers and jewelers.

Watchmaker Georges-Auguste Leschot joined the company in 1839 and invented the pantograph watch movement. Vacheron Constantin's famous Maltese Cross logo appeared in 1880. In 1885, the company launched the first nonmagnetic watch. Vacheron Constantin opened their first dedicated shop in Geneva in 1906.

Vacheron Constantin introduced an ultra-thin wristwatch in 1955. In 1970 the company dropped the "&" from its name. Its famous asymmetrical signature model was launched in 1972 and the exquisite Kallista watch followed in 1979. This extraordinary timepiece was carved from a single gold ingot and decorated with one-hundred-and-thirty carats of diamonds. It is reputed to be the most valuable watch in the world. In 1994 the company launched its remarkable Gerhard Kremer commemorative watch with its unique compass-like hands.

Vacheron Constantin was bought by the Richemont luxury goods group in 1996. Its current range of watches includes the Patrimony, Malte, 1972, and Historique collections. Its timepieces are equipped with mechanical, automatic, and quartz movements. In 2004 the company moved to purpose-built headquarters in Plan-les-Ouates, Geneva. The company now creates around twenty-thousand prestige watches each year including specially commissioned watches.

(above) Vacheron Constantin Malte Big Date. 18K white gold. Water-resistant, self-winding. 2005.
*Courtesy of Antiquorum Auctioneers*

(above) Vacheron Constantin Patrimony Contemporary. Manual wind. White gold, silver dial. Current.

(right) Vacheron Constantin. Thin, 18K yellow gold. Stepped bezel. Center seconds. 1960s.
*Courtesy of Antiquorum Auctioneers*

(below) Vacheron Constantin. Manual wind, water-resistant. Rose gold, silver dial. Current.

THE ILLUSTRATED DIRECTORY OF WATCHES

(left) Vacheron Constantin Patrimony Excellence Platinum. Thin. 2006.

*Courtesy of Antiquorum Auctioneers*

(below) Vacheron Constantin. 18K yellow gold, crab lugs. Guilloche silver dial, Arabic quarters. 1950s.

*Courtesy of Antiquorum Auctioneers*

(above and left) Vacheron Constantin Patrimony Bi-Retrograde Day and Date. 18K pink gold, silver opaline dial. Current.

(left) Vacheron Constantin stainless steel round-button chronograph. Large date. Self-winding, water-resistant. 2000s.

*Courtesy of Antiquorum Auctioneers*

(below) Vacheron Constantin Jubilee 240. 18K white gold, tonneau-shaped. 1995.

*Courtesy of Antiquorum Auctioneers*

(right) Vacheron Constantin Overseas automatic. Stainless steel, silver guilloche dial. Luminous hands. Current.

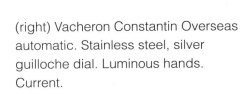

(right) Vacheron Constantin Overseas Chronograph. 18K rose gold, silver dial. Current.

(right) Vacheron Constantin steel and 18K pink gold. Concave bezel, roman numerals. 1940s.

*Courtesy of Antiquorum Auctioneers*

(above) Vacheron Constantin skeletonized. Midsized. 18K white gold, diamond-set bezel. 1980s.

*Courtesy of Antiquorum Auctioneers*

(right) Vacheron Constantin Malte Tonneau chronograph. 18K rose gold, silver guilloche dial. Current.

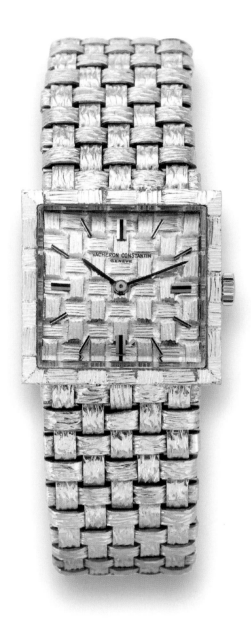

(below) Vacheron Constantin
Golden Square. 18K white
gold and diamonds, woven
bracelet. 1970s.
*Courtesy of Antiquorum Auctioneers*

(above) Vacheron Constantin. 18K
white gold, integrated woven link
bracelet. 1970.
*Courtesy of Antiquorum Auctioneers*

(above) Vacheron Constantin,
case by Ferdinand Verger.
Platinum and diamonds. 1916.
*Courtesy of Antiquorum Auctioneers*

(left and right)
Vacheron Constantin
Metiers d'Art,
Perspectives d'Art
Dove for Only
Watch. 18K white
gold and diamonds.
2011.
*Courtesy of Antiquorum*
*Auctioneers*

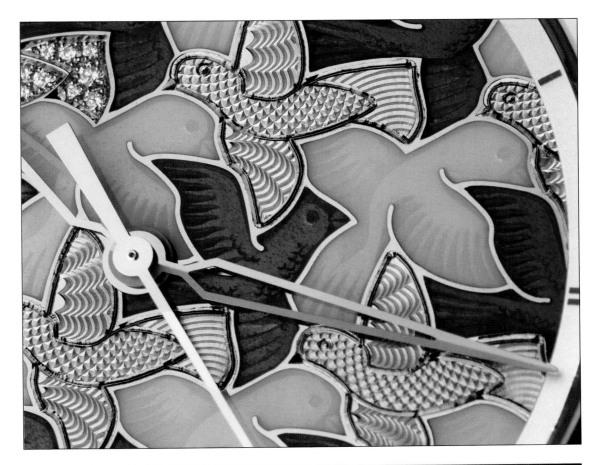

(right) Vacheron Constantin 1972 Cambree. Asymmetric and curved. 18K pink gold and diamonds. 1972.
*Courtesy of Antiquorum Auctioneers*

(below) Vacheron Constantin. 18K yellow gold, square. 1954.
*Courtesy of Antiquorum Auctioneers*

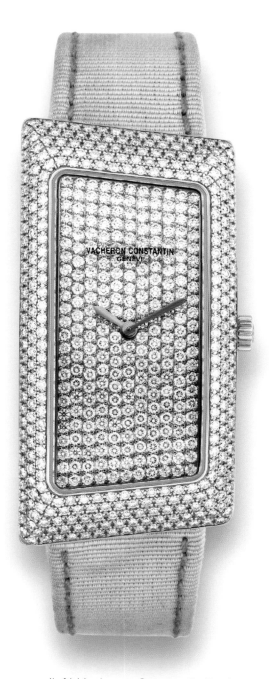

(left) Vacheron Constantin Patrimony Traditionelle quartz. 18K white gold. Diamond-set dial, bezel, and lugs. Current.

(right) Vacheron Constantin Saltarello automatic, jump hour. Limited edition. 18K pink gold, cushion-shaped. 1999.
*Courtesy of Antiquorum Auctioneers*

(left and below) Vacheron Constantin Historiques American 1921. 18K rose gold, silver dial. Subsidiary seconds. Current.

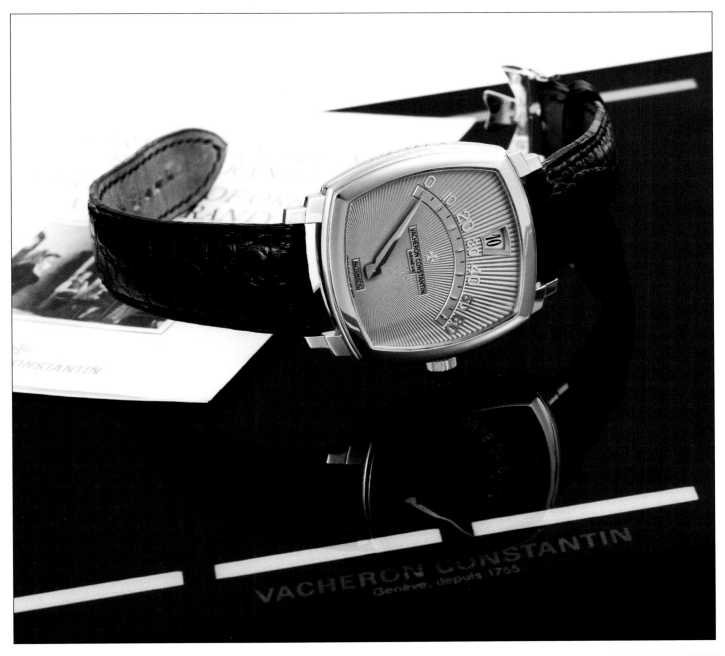

(left) Vacheron Constantin.
White gold, cushion-shaped.
White dial, Breguet
numerals. 1920s.
*Courtesy of Antiquorum Auctioneers*

(right) Vacheron Constantin.
18K yellow gold. Black dial,
triangular indexes. 1950s.
*Courtesy of Antiquorum Auctioneers*

(left) Vacheron
Constantin Patrimony
Traditionelle quartz.
18K white gold dress
watch. Dial pave-set
with diamonds.
Current.

(above) Vacheron Constantin Malte Retrograde, date. Limited edition. Platinum, skeletonized. 2002.

*Courtesy of Antiquorum Auctioneers*

(above) Vacheron Constantin Patrimony Traditionelle automatic. 18K white gold, diamond-set bezel. Current.

(below) Vacheron Constantin Patrimony Traditionelle skeletonized automatic. 18K white gold, diamond-set bezel. Current.

(left) Vacheron Constantin Malte Tourbillon. 18K pink gold. Tonneau-shaped. 2001.
*Courtesy of Antiquorum Auctioneers*

(below) Vacheron Constantin octagonal. 18K yellow gold. Dial and bracelet pave-set with diamonds and rubies. 1990s.

(above) Vacheron Constantin. Square, platinum. Diamond indexes. 1951.
*Courtesy of Antiquorum Auctioneers*

(left) Vacheron Constantin Les Historiques square-button chronograph. 18K yellow gold. 2002.

*Courtesy of Antiquorum Auctioneers*

(right) Vacheron Constantin Toledo 1952 moon phases. Rectangular, curved sides. Guilloche silver dial. Current.

(left) Vacheron Constantin Patrimony Traditionelle quartz. 18K white gold, silver dial. Diamond-set bezel. Current.

(right) Vacheron Constantin Mercator. 18K yellow gold. 22K yellow gold dial engraved with map of the continents. Marine compass hands. 1996.

*Courtesy of Antiquorum Auctioneers*

(below) Vacheron Constantin Cornes de Vaches round-button chronograph. 18K yellow gold. Flat bezel. 1960.

*Courtesy of Antiquorum Auctioneers*

(above) Vacheron Constantin. All-diamond watch set with twenty-three carats. 1991.

*Courtesy of Antiquorum Auctioneers*

# Van Cleef & Arpels

Estelle Arpels and Alfred Van Cleef were married in 1896. They both came from families of French diamond merchants. Alfred collaborated with his brother-in-law Charles Arpels and in 1906 the partners opened their store at 22 Place Vendome, Paris. This was a very exclusive area in the heart of Paris, just opposite the luxurious Ritz hotel. Although Van Cleef & Arpels began as a jeweler, the company started to offer watches in the 1910s. At this time, the company specialized in bracelet watches but also produced the first watch with a leather strap in 1923. Van Cleef's daughter Renee Puissant designed many pieces for the family company. In 1939 Claude Arpels opened a boutique in New York's Rockefeller Center. A few years later, the shop moved to 744 Fifth Avenue. Van Cleef & Arpels has introduced many iconic watch collections including the Cadenas, Alhambra, Charms, and Carrelage. Descendants of several early lines are still in production. In 1972 the company opened the Pierre Arpels Boutique des Heures in Place Vendome. This store was dedicated to the sale of Van Cleef & Arpels watches. Over the years, Van Cleef & Arpels has developed a lavish and exquisite style of work. Their watches are decorated with many of the jeweler's arts, including enameling, inlay, and even sculpture. The company motto is "The poetry of time" and their watches are far more than functional timepieces.

Many high-profile celebrities have worn Van Cleef & Arpels watches including Princess Grace of Monaco, Maria Callas, Audrey Hepburn, the Duchess of Windsor, and Sophia Loren.

Van Cleef & Arpels is now part of the Richemont group.

(left and right) Van Cleef & Arpels Damen Mini quartz. 18K yellow gold and diamonds. Sapphire crystal. Vintage.

(below) Van Cleef & Arpels Sportsman Le Chronographe. Automatic. Three sub-dials. Stainless steel, cream dial. Circa 2006.

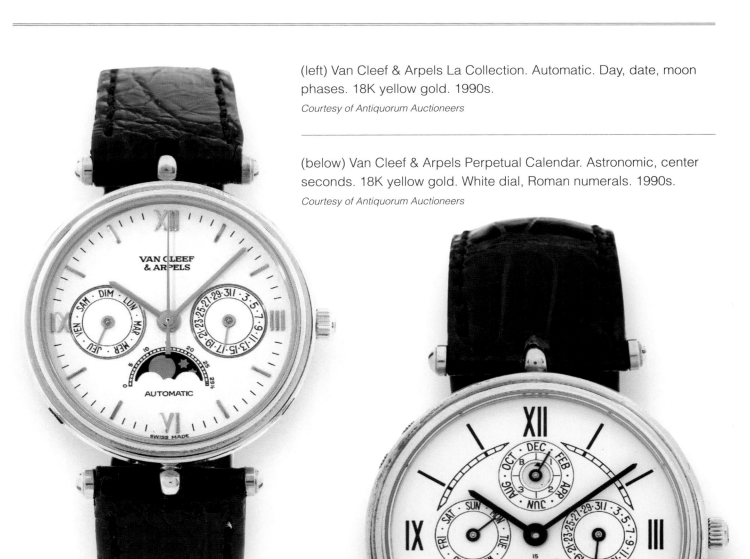

(left) Van Cleef & Arpels La Collection. Automatic. Day, date, moon phases. 18K yellow gold. 1990s.
*Courtesy of Antiquorum Auctioneers*

(below) Van Cleef & Arpels Perpetual Calendar. Astronomic, center seconds. 18K yellow gold. White dial, Roman numerals. 1990s.
*Courtesy of Antiquorum Auctioneers*

(left) Van Cleef & Arpels Roma. 18K yellow gold, leather strap. Quartz.

(left) Van Cleef & Arpels Alhambra Charms. Motif modeled on the four-leafed clover. Each leaf represents health, wealth, true love, and good luck.

(below) Van Cleef & Arpels Lady Arpels Fairy for Only Watch. 18K white gold and diamonds. Purple guilloche enamel dial. 2007.

*Courtesy of Antiquorum Auctioneers*

(above) Van Cleef & Arpels automatic. Day, night, moon phases. 18K yellow gold and steel. 1990s.

*Courtesy of Antiquorum Auctioneers*

(above) Van Cleef & Arpels
Midnight Tourbillon Nacre.
18K white gold. Tourbillon
movement. 2010.

(right) Van Cleef & Arpels
Monsieur Arpels Flying
Tourbillon. Limited edition.
18K pink gold and diamonds.
Visible, one-minute tourbillon
regulator. Mother-of-pearl
dial. Circa 2000.
*Courtesy of Antiquorum Auctioneers*

(left) Van Cleef & Arpels skeleton. 18K yellow gold and diamonds. Vendome-type lugs. 1980s.

*Courtesy of Antiquorum Auctioneers*

(below) Van Cleef & Arpels Squelette. Skeletonized 18K yellow gold and diamonds. Matching diamond-set buckle. Circa 1990.

*Courtesy of Antiquorum Auctioneers*

(left) Van Cleef & Arpels Poetic Complications Pont des Amoureux. Retrograde mechanical movement. 18K white gold and diamonds. Contre-jour enamel dial. 2010.

(right) Van Cleef & Arpels African Hippopotamus. White gold and diamonds. Sculptural enamel dial inlaid with diamonds and mother-of-pearl.

(above) Van Cleef & Arpels World Time Alarm. Limited edition. 18K yellow gold. Ivory-colored dial. Center seconds. 1997.
*Courtesy of Antiquorum Auctioneers*

(right) Van Cleef & Arpels Poetic Complications, Poetic Wish Lady featuring Notre Dame, Paris. Three-dimensional hand-painted mother-of-pearl dial.

(above) Van Cleef & Arpels Poetic Complications, Les Voyages Extraordinaire. From the Earth to the Moon. The 18K white gold star indicates the hours; the space ship indicates the minutes. 2011.

(right) Van Cleef & Arpels Poetic Complications, Five Weeks in a Balloon. Homage to Jules Verne. Mechanical. White gold. Enamel and mother-of-pearl dial. Automaton indicators.

(above) Van Cleef & Arpels Lady Arpels Polar Landscape. White gold and diamonds. Sculptural enamel dial inlaid with diamonds and mother-of-pearl. 2011.

(below and right) Van Cleef & Arpels Poetic Complications, Poetic Midnight Wish featuring the Eiffel Tower, Paris. 18K white gold and diamonds. Hand-painted dial. Highly decorative movement.

(above) Van Cleef & Arpels Les Voyages Extraordinaire. Homage to Jules Verne. 18K white gold, automaton hands. 2001.

# *Vulcain*

Vulcain was founded by the Ditisheim brothers in 1858. It was located in the Swiss watch making village of La Chaux-de-Fonds. The most important breakthrough in the company history was the invention of the first wristwatch alarm in 1947. Vulcain's Cricket was the first watch to have an alarm loud enough to wake the wearer.

Vulcain watches became popular with several United States presidents, beginning with Harry S. Truman. This earned Vulcain the motto "The watch for Presidents." President Barack Obama wears a Vulcain watch and the company has launched a commemorative model in his honor. Vulcain's Cricket watch also earned a reputation for ruggedness. They were worn by the Italian party that conquered K2 in 1954.

Vulcain now manufactures seven different Cricket movements. These are all mechanical but some are hand-wound and some are automatic. Vulcain also has a reputation for its superb cloisonné enamel work.

The company launched the Imperial Gong watch in 2005. This was another milestone watch for Vulcain, equipped with both a tourbillon movement and an alarm.

Vulcain is now based in Le Locle, Switzerland and continues to manufacture an extensive range of prestige models.

(above) Vulcain Anniversary Heart. Alarm. Cricket caliber V-18. 18K pink gold.

(left) Vulcain Nautical Heritage diver's watch. Rotating bezel with decompression stops. Alarm audible underwater. 2011.

(right) Vulcain Cricket Dual Time. Alarm. Stainless steel. 2005.
*Courtesy of Antiquorum Auctioneers*

(below) Vulcain Aviator GMT steel chronograph. Cricket caliber V-10. Stainless steel.

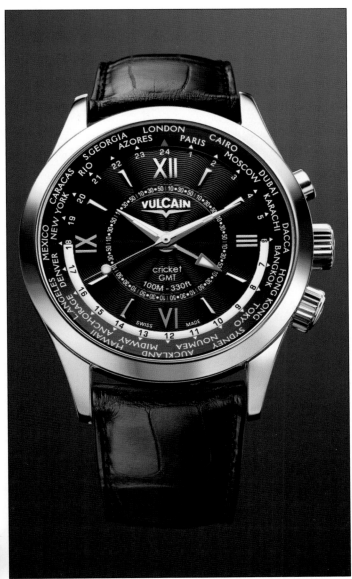

(left) Vulcain Cricket Anniversary Heart President. Alarm. Limited edition. 2010.

(right) Vulcain Vulcanographe, date. Gold. Two subsidiary dials.

(below) Vulcain Golden Voice Lady. Stainless steel. Center seconds.

(left) Vulcain President Barack Obama. Stainless steel chronograph. Alarm.

(above) Vulcain Around the World. World time chronograph, alarm. Stainless steel and enamel.

(left) Vulcain Anniversary Heart automatic.

(above) Vulcain Cricket GMT World Time Aeropostale. Alarm. Limited edition. Pink gold, cloisonné dial. 2011.
*Courtesy of Antiquorum Auctioneers*

(right) Vulcain Skeleton Cricket for Only Watch. Alarm. 18K pink gold. 2011.
*Courtesy of Antiquorum Auctioneers*

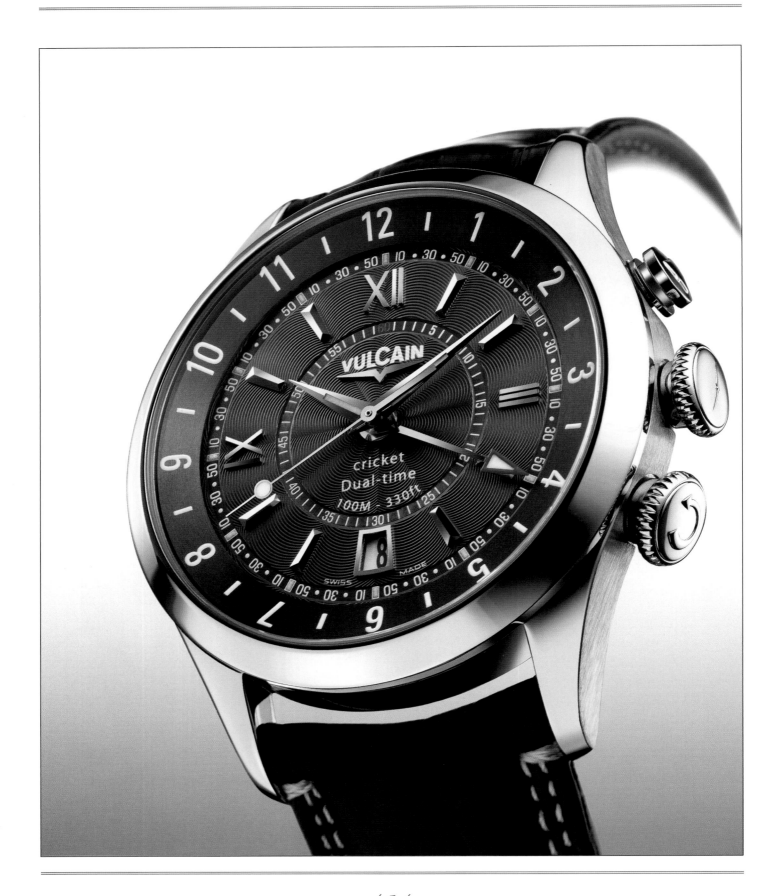

(left) Vulcain Dual Time, date. Cricket movement. Stainless steel, water-resistant.

(right) Vulcain GMT Dragon World Time. Cricket caliber V-13. Pink gold, water-resistant.

(below) Vulcain Cricket Diver X-Treme. Gold. Water-resistant.

(right) Vulcain Cloisonné The Pandas. Cricket caliber V-13. 18K pink gold.

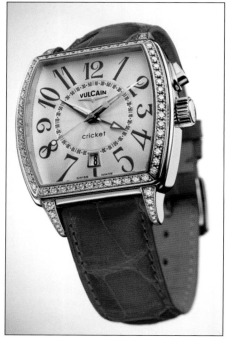

(above) Vulcain Millesime 1928.
Manual wind. Steel and diamonds.

(aleft) Vulcain Cricket GMT World
Time Concord. Alarm. Large, 18K
pink gold, cloisonné dial 2011.

*Courtesy of Antiquorum Auctioneers*

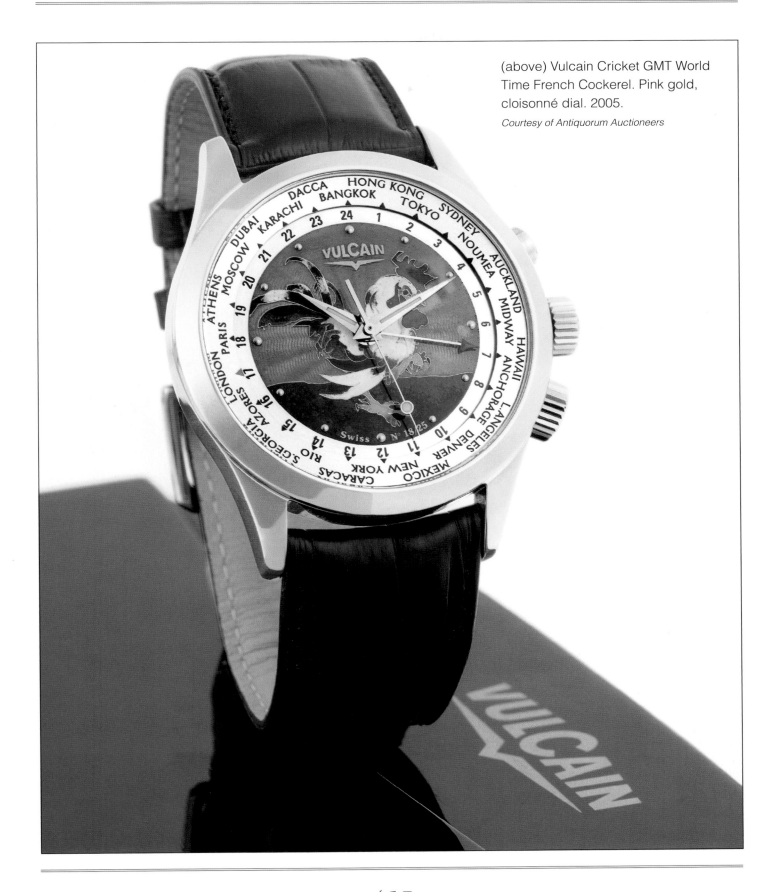

(above) Vulcain Cricket GMT World Time French Cockerel. Pink gold, cloisonné dial. 2005.

*Courtesy of Antiquorum Auctioneers*

(left) Vulcain At the Races. Alarm. Cloisonné enamel.

(below) Vulcain Cricket watch. Cloisonné enamel.

(right) Vulcain Cricket Classic 1951. Alarm. Pink gold. 2008.

*Courtesy of Antiquorum Auctioneers*

# *Wakmann*

The Wakmann Watch Company was founded in New York City too import watches and movements into the American market. It was listed on the New York stock exchange. Wakmann specialized in Swiss watches and movements and the company's reputation for reliability grew. As well as importing movements from Valjoux, Lemania, and Landeron, Wakmann also assembled their own watches. The company specialized in high-quality stopwatches, chronographs, Braille watches, dress watches, and aviation instruments. Wakmann also collaborated with other prestige watchmakers, including Breitling. One of the company's best-known models was the Chronomat with its built-in circular slide rule.

Wakmann's advertising slogan was "For the time of your life." The company had some success and became a supplier to the United States military. But ultimately, Wakmann was taken over by its more successful collaborator Breitling.

(above) Wakmann automatic chronograph. Date. Gold-plated.

(right) Wakmann triple-date chronograph. Mechanical, manual wind. Vintage.

(below) Wakmann Braille watch. White dial with raised dots and Arabic numerals. Hinged crystal. Vintage.

(above) Wakmann Swiss-made round button chronograph. Self-winding, automatic. Tonneau-shaped. Stainless steel and gold plate. 1980s.

*Courtesy of Antiquorum Auctioneers*

(above and below) Wakmann two-dial chronograph. Manual wind. Cushion-shaped. Gold-topped, gold dial. 1970s.

(left) Wakmann triple-date chronograph. Antimagnetic. Stainless steel and gold plate. 1970s.

*Courtesy of Antiquorum Auctioneers*

# Waltham

Waltham was founded in 1850 and can claim to be America's oldest watch making company. It was the brainchild of three partners, Aaron Denison, Edward Howard, and David Davis. The trio wanted to make timepieces for the masses. They established their business in Roxbury, Massachusetts, but moved to Waltham, Massachusetts in 1854. It was here that the company built an industrial-scale watch factory, fully equipped for mass production. In 1863, Waltham presented a Waltham Model 1857 pocket watch to President Abraham Lincoln to commemorate his Gettysburg Address.

In 1870 Waltham launched the Crescent Street railroad watch which was to become one of its most important models. The company's first watch for women, the Lady Waltham appeared in 1912. Between 1850 and 1957 the company changed its name and identity at least nine times. Finally Waltham decided to relocate its business to Lausanne in Switzerland. Waltham had manufactured over forty million timepieces and precision instruments during its time in Massachusetts. Its new strategy was to make a smaller number of more prestigious and expensive watches. Many Waltham Swiss-made watches were exported back to the United States and were worn by many famous Americans. In 1971 astronaut David Scott the commander of the Apollo 15 mission wore his Waltham watch during a moonwalk, after his Omega Speedmaster was damaged. In 1990 Frank Sinatra wore the diamond-encrusted Waltham Radiant 2000 at a concert he gave at the Hotel Imperial in Tokyo, Japan. At the time the Radiant 2000 was reputed to be the world's most expensive wristwatch.

Waltham International is currently located in Marin-Epagnier, Switzerland and its main export market is Japan. Its current model line-up includes the Lord Waltham, Lone Eagle, Fidalgo, Lady Baroda, and LW34 Lune watches. A twenty-first-century version of the iconic Waltham Crescent was launched at 2010's BaselWorld watch and jewelry fair.

(above) Waltham Hi-Beat. Silver sunburst dial. Chrome-plated steel. Oversized crown.

(below) Waltham RCAF pilot's watch for the Royal Canadian Air Force. Chrome and stainless steel. 1942.
*Trebor's Vintage Watches*

(above) Waltham dress watch. Manual wind. Plain black dial set with a single diamond. Circa 1980s.
*Trebor's Vintage Watches*

(above) Waltham diver's watch. Incabloc shock protection. Center seconds. 1969.

(above) Waltham engraved watch face. Gold-plated. 1923.

(righ) Waltham three-dial chronograph. Incabloc shock protection. Stainless steel. Vintage.

(above and right) Waltham Swissonic Swiss-made watch. Vintage.

(below) Waltham three-dial chronograph. Center seconds. Stainless steel.

(above) Waltham triangular Masonic watch. Gold-filed. Bezel and circular lug decorated with Masonic symbols. 1950s.

*Courtesy of Antiquorum Auctioneers*

(below) Waltham automatic. Stainless steel. Sleek dial, baton indexes, gold hands. 1969.

(above) Waltham skeletonized, cushion-shaped watch. Stainless steel.

*Courtesy of Antiquorum Auctioneers*

(above) Waltham transitional strap watch. Manual wind. Gold-filled. 1914.

*Trebor's Vintage Watches*

(above) Waltham gold tone. Baton indexes, center seconds. Vintage.

(right) Waltham Tank watch. 1940s.

(above) Waltham Premier curvex. Gold-plated. 1930s.

# West End Watch Co.

Alcide Droz & Sons was founded in 1864. The company was based in St. Imier, Switzerland. The company claims to have developed the first-ever waterproof watch. In 1886, Alcide Droz & Sons produced the first West End branded watch for the Indian market. The West End Watch Co. counts this as its foundation date. The company produced watches for the British armed forces in World War One. In 1934 West End was the first watch making company to use the Incabloc anti-shock system. West End watches were notoriously rugged and one went to the top of Everest with the Chinese Expedition of 1960.

The West End Watch Co. now specializes in exporting to the Middle and Far East markets. Its current wristwatch collections include the Silk Road, Sowar 1916, Trafalgar Square, and Sowar Chronograph. The company is now based in Leytron, Switzerland.

(left) West End Sowar automatic. Gold. Day/date indicators. Arabic numbers. Current.

(below) West End Sowar military-style automatic. Day/date indicators. Fabric strap. Vintage.

(above) West End Secundus from World War I. Subsidiary seconds. Wire lug. Vintage.

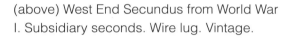

(right) West End Sowar automatic chronometer. Stainless steel and gold. Current.

(above) West End Queen Anne manual wind. Nickel case. Subsidiary seconds. Vintage.

*littlecogs.com*

(left) West End manual wind. Subsidiary seconds. Enamel dial. Vintage.

*littlecogs.com*

(right) West End Sowar automatic all gold. Sapphire crystal. Water-resistant. Current.

(above) West End Sowar automatic. Stainless steel, black dial. Large crown. Current.

(below) West End chrome. Manual wind. Center seconds. Vintage.

*littlecogs.com*

(above) West End Sowar Prima automatic chronograph. Stainless steel. Arabic days of the week. Vintage.

(left) West End Sowar automatic. Stainless steel. Integral bracelet. Current.

(left and above) West End Sowar automatic. Stainless steel large bar lugs. Subsidiary seconds. Date. Transparent case back. Current.

(left and right) West End Sowar stainless steel. Black dial. Day/date indicators. Current.

(lbelow) West End stainless steel. Manual wind. Subsidiary seconds. Vintage.

*littlecogs.com*

# *Wittnauer*

Wittnauer was established in New York City in 1890 by Albert Wittnauer. Wittnauer was a Swiss immigrant who arrived in New York City in 1872. From the beginning the company concentrated on professional quality timepieces for astronomers, explorers, and navigators. Wittnauer also made watches for United States army and navy personnel. Wittnauer created the "All Proof" watch in 1918. This model became especially popular with aviators. Amelia Earhart wore a Wittnauer when setting her flight records.

Wittnauer is now owned by Bulova who keep the Wittnauer trade name alive.

(left) Wittnauer chronograph. Stainless steel. Screw back. 1950s.

*Trebor's Vintage Watches*

(left) Wittnauer automatic. Textured dial. Yellow gold-plated. 1960s.

*Trebor's Vintage Watches*

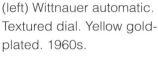

(right) Wittnauer crosshair-patterned dial. Stainless steel. Screw back. 1960s.

*Trebor's Vintage Watches*

(left) Wittnauer Weems. 14K yellow gold. 1950s.

*Courtesy of Antiquorum Auctioneers*

(right) Wittnauer Revue. Manual wind. Pink gold-topped. Vintage.

*littlecogs.com*

(below) Wittnauer. Unusual rounded square-shaped case. Stainless steel and diamonds, integral bracelet. Vintage.

(right) Wittnauer Electro-Chron electronic. Stainless steel. Presented to Joe DiMaggio in 1962.

*Courtesy of Antiquorum Auctioneers*

(below) Wittnauer Super-Compressor self-winding automatic. Stainless steel 1965.

*Courtesy of Antiquorum Auctioneers*

(above) Wittnauer round-button chronograph. Two sub-dials. Stainless steel. 1950s.

*Courtesy of Antiquorum Auctioneers*

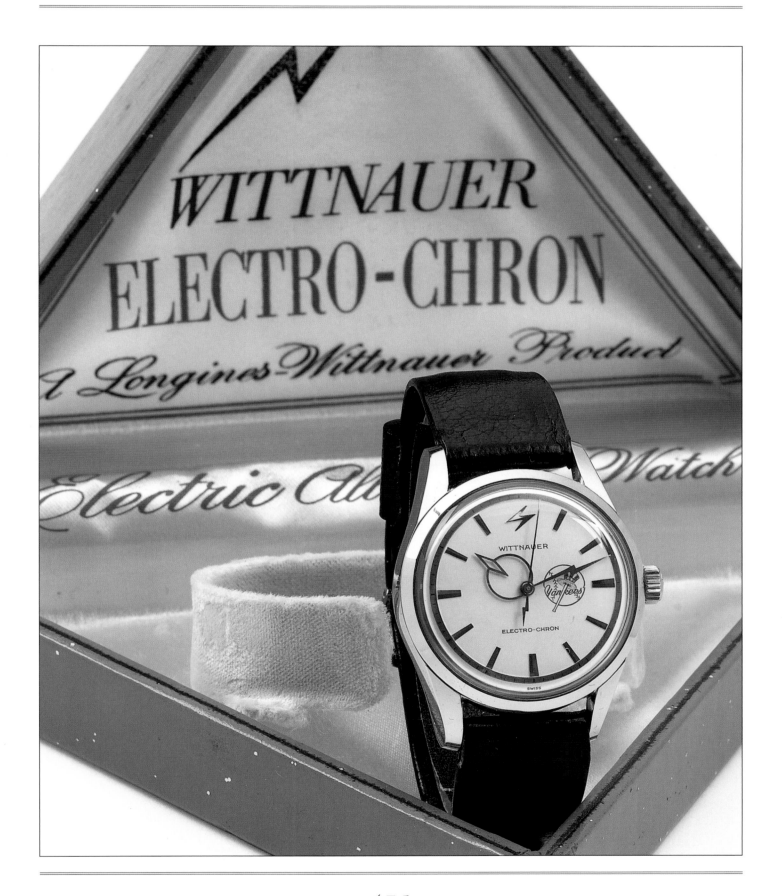

(left) Wittnauer chronograph. Stainless steel. Luminous hands, triangular indexes. 1950s.

(right) Wittnauer quartz. 2006.

*Trebor's Vintage Watches*

(below) Wittnauer three-dial chronograph. Stainless steel, black dial. Black and orange rotating bezel. Vintage.

(above) Wittnauer dress watch. 14K yellow gold. 1960s.

*Trebor's Vintage Watches*

(above) Wittnauer automatic. Textured dial. Stainless steel. Circa 1965.

(left) Wittnauer professional chronograph. Two sub-dials. Revolving bezel. Stainless steel.

(right) Wittnauer Mystery dial automatic. Stainless steel. Waterproof. 1960s.

*Trebor's Vintage Watches*

(above) Wittnauer manual wind. Tank-shaped, white gold-filled. Black dial. Vintage.

(right) Wittnauer gold-plated automatic. Center seconds, screw back. Vintage.

littlecogs.com

# *Wyler*

Swiss watchmaker Paul Wyler established Wyler in 1923. His factory was located in Biel, Switzerland. The company became immediately well-known for its Incaflex shock protection system. The effectiveness of this invention was proved in 1956 when two Wyler Incaflex watches were dropped from the top of the Eiffel Tower in Paris. Both watches survived in good working order. Wyler launched the Unbreakable in 1930. In 1937 the company introduced its own waterproof system that relied on hydraulic sealing.

The Wyler brand name fell out of view after 1972. It was relaunched at the Baselworld watch and jewelry fair of 2007. Wyler's new range consisted of striking-looking chronographs in large tonneau-shaped cases. These were constructed in various modern materials including ceramic and titanium. Unfortunately Wyler's business was badly affected by the economic crisis of 2009. The company closed its doors in November, 2009.

(above) Wyler Incaflex. Stainless steel, silver dial. 1960s.

(left) Wyler Code R chronograph. Pink gold, titanium, and carbon fiber. 2009.

*Courtesy of Antiquorum Auctioneers*

(below) Wyler Code R chronometer. Pink gold, titanium, and carbon fiber. Curved, tonneau-shaped. 2009.

*Courtesy of Antiquorum Auctioneers*

(left) Wyler Incaflex. Waterproof, antimagnetic. Chrome and stainless steel. 1940s.

*Trebor's Vintage Watches*

(above) Wyler Code R Incaflex chronograph. Titanium, carbon fiber. 2009.

*Courtesy of Antiquorum Auctioneers*

(left) Wyler Incaflex Dynawind automatic. Stainless steel. 1960s.

*Trebor's Vintage Watches*

(right) Wyler Code R Flying Tourbillon GMT. Titanium, carbon fiber. 2010.

*Courtesy of Antiquorum Auctioneers*

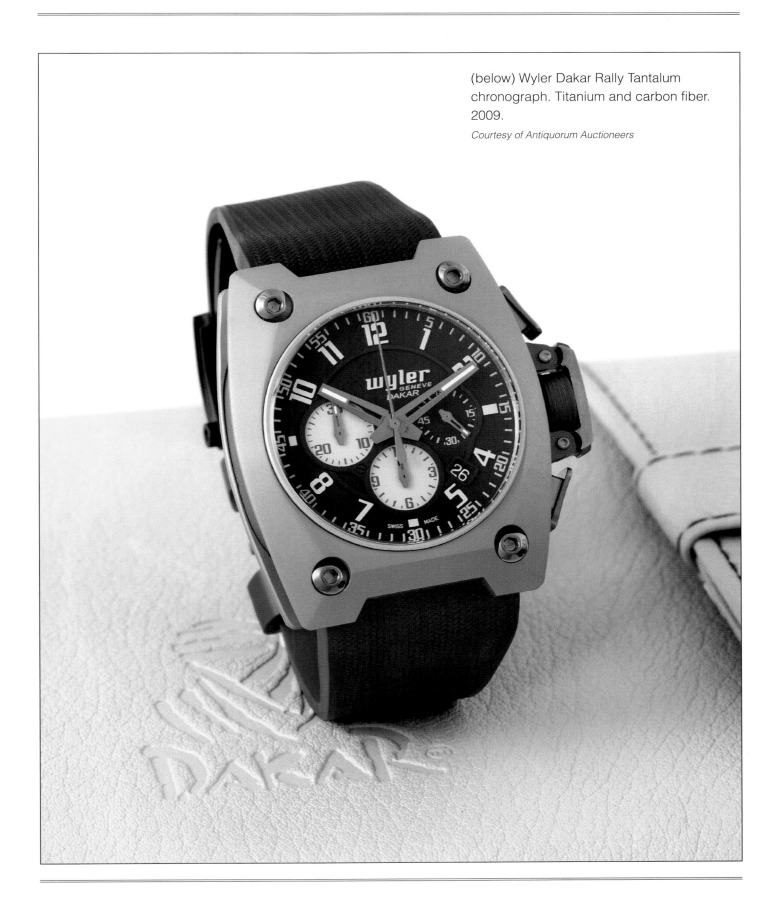

(below) Wyler Dakar Rally Tantalum
chronograph. Titanium and carbon fiber.
2009.

*Courtesy of Antiquorum Auctioneers*

(right) Wyler manual.
Subsidiary seconds.
Vintage.

*littlecogs.com*

(right) Wyler Incaflex Dynawind automatic, date.
Stainless steel, gold-plated bezel. Late 1960s.

(above) Wyler chronograph. Titanium and
carbon fiber. 2009.

*Courtesy of Antiquorum Auctioneers*

(right) Wyler Code S. Stainless steel,
titanium, and carbon fiber. 2009.

*Courtesy of Antiquorum Auctioneers*

(right) Wyler Incaflex. Manual wind. Vintage.

(left) Wyler Code R Incaflex. Titanium and carbon fiber. Large, tonneau-shaped. 2009.
*Courtesy of Antiquorum Auctioneers*

(above) Wyler gold sports watch. Incaflex shock protection. 2007.

(right) Wyler Incaflex. Monocoque case. Water-resistant. Circa 1950.

# Zenith

Georges Favre-Jacot established his business in Le Locle, Switzerland in 1865. In his search for accuracy Favre-Jacot decided to build his own factory rather than sourcing watch parts from local craftspeople. He produced his first pocket chronograph in 1899. In 1911 the business was re-named Zenith. The company prospered and had over two thousand employees in by 1925. Zenith launched its famous Caliber 135 movement in 1948 and the Caliber 501 1K in 1960. Its most iconic movement, the El Primero followed in 1969. At the time it was the world's most precise chronograph movement. The El Primero went out of production during the quartz crisis of the 1970s. Zenith was forced to produce quartz watches to compete with cheap imports. The El Primero was re-introduced in 1984. Zenith's ultra-thin Elite automatic movement followed in 1994.

Zenith joined the LVMH group in 2000. The company headquarters are still in Le Locle, Switzerland.

Several very famous people have worn Zenith watches including Roald Amundsen and Mahatma Gandhi. Mahatma Gandhi's Zenith was sold at auction in New York for 1.8 million dollars.

(left) Zenith El Primero automatic. 18K rose gold. Diamond-set bezel and hour markers. Mother-of-pearl dial.

(above) Zenith chronograph. Pink gold. 1950s.

*Courtesy of Antiquorum Auctioneers*

(right) Zenith Grande Class El Primero chronograph automatic. Stainless steel. 2008.

*Courtesy of Antiquorum Auctioneers*

(above) Zenith Defy Extreme. High-pressure-resistant chronograph.
Titanium, oversized. 2007.

*Courtesy of Antiquorum Auctioneers*

(right) Zenith Defy Classic Chrono Aero. El Primero automatic.
Oversized. 2007.

*Courtesy of Antiquorum Auctioneers*

(below) Zenith El Primero Chronomaster square-button chronograph. Stainless steel. 2003.
*Courtesy of Antiquorum Auctioneers*

(above) Zenith Espada Luna automatic chronograph. 18K yellow gold. 1970s.
*Courtesy of Antiquorum Auctioneers*

(left) Zenith Chronomaster El Primero automatic. Yellow gold. 1980s.
*Courtesy of Antiquorum Auctioneers*

(above) Zenith Grande Class El Primero chronograph. 18K white gold. 2000s.

*Courtesy of Antiquorum Auctioneers*

(right) Zenith Espada Sub Sea automatic
chronograph. Astronomic, moon phases.
Stainless steel. 1970s.
*Courtesy of Antiquorum Auctioneers*

(below) Zenith Port Royal El Primero
automatic chronograph. PVD-coated titanium.
Copper-colored dial. 2007.
*Courtesy of Antiquorum Auctioneers*

(right) Zenith El Primero square-button chronograph. Stainless steel. 2000.

*Courtesy of Antiquorum Auctioneers*

(left) Zenith manual
wind. 18K yellow
gold. Circa 1950s.

(below) Zenith Elite
681 ultra-thin.
Subsidiary seconds.
18K rose gold.

(left) Zenith manual. Gold-plated. Vintage.

(above and left) Zenith El Primero Chronomaster Open Grande. Date, moon phases, sun phases. 18K rose gold or stainless steel. Black or silver dial. 2012.

(right) Zenith manual wind. Subsidiary seconds. 18K rose gold. 1950s.

*Trebor's Vintage Watches*

(above) Zenith Espada El Primero. Date. Stainless steel. Current.

(right) Zenith hexagonal. 9K rose gold. Circa 1937.

*Courtesy of Antiquorum Auctioneers*

(left) Zenith Prime Caliber 420 chronograph. Stainless steel. White dial, exhibition back. Vintage.

(below) Zenith Captain. Hammer automatic. Gold-filled. Circa 1950s.
*Trebor's Vintage Watches*

(above) Zenith 28800 Sporto manual wind. Gold-topped. Circa 1970s.
*Trebor's Vintage Watches*

(right) Zenith two-dial chronometer. Center seconds. 1950s.

(right, below and bottom) Zenith Elite Captain chronograph. Stainless steel or 18K rose gold. Black or silver sunray dial.

(right) Zenith Elite ultra-thin. 18K rose gold. Exhibition back. Current.

(left) Zenith Academy Christopher Columbus Equation du Temps. 18K rose gold. 2011.

(below) Zenith Elite ultra-thin. Stainless steel.

(left and below) Zenith Captain Winsor Annual Calendar El Primero. 18K rose gold or stainless steel.

# *Zodiac*

Ariste Calame wanted to create the most accurate watch in the world. He established his watch making company in Le Locle, Switzerland in 1882. The company patented the Zodiac trademark in 1930. In the same year the company introduced the Zodiac anti-shock system and the company's first automatic movement. The Beta 21 caliber followed in 1932. This was one of the first Swiss analog quartz movements. Zodiac introduced several famous models. The Autographic appeared in 1949, the Sea Wolf diver's watch in 1953, the Aerospace in 1960, and the Aerospace Jet in 1962. Zodiac introduced the Dynotron in 1968, which was the first Swiss electronic watch. The iconic Astrographic with its floating hour and minute hands followed in 1969. Zodiac launched the Olympus in 1970 and the LCD chronometer in 1977.

In 2001 Zodiac was acquired by Fossil Inc.. Zodiac now makes fashionable diving, aviation, and race watches at accessible prices. The company introduced the Sea Dragon and V-Wolf in 2004, the Zodiac Mission Extreme in 2007, and the ZMX-05 deep sea diver's watch in 2010.

(below) Zodiac triple date calendar automatic. Stainless steel and gold-plate. 1960s.

*Courtesy of Antiquorum Auctioneers*

(above) Zodiac Sea-Chron 20 ATM diver's watch. Stainless steel. 1960s.

*Courtesy of Antiquorum Auctioneers*

(right) Zodiac Sea Wolf automatic. Early orange-accented Sea Wolf diver's watch.

(left) Zodiac three-button chronograph. Center seconds. Stainless steel. Vintage.

(left) Zodiac oversized diver's watch. Stainless steel.

(right) Zodiac Custom. Military-style. Stainless steel, black dial.

(below) Zodiac Adventure Sport ZO7901 diver's watch. Current.

(right) Zodiac Autographic automatic. Stainless steel. Honeycomb dial. 1960s.

*Trebor's Vintage Watches*

(left) Zodiac Sea-Chron diver's watch. Stainless steel, black dial.

(below) Zodiac Sea Wolf. Stainless steel, revolving bezel. Vintage.

(left) Zodiac Aerospace GMT Datographic. Automatic diver's watch. 1960s.

*Trebor's Vintage Watches*

(above) Zodiac three-hand quartz diver's watch for deep water. Uni-directional bezel.

(left) Zodiac Adventure Sport ZO5500 diver's watch.

# Acknowledgements

This book could not have been produced without the kind and generous cooperation of the following auction houses, watch retailers, and private collectors. Some of those who assisted in this way have asked to remain anonymous; the others include:

**Antiquorum Auctioneers**
www.antiquorum.com
595 Madison Avenue
New York, NY 10022
United States of America
212-750-1103

**Robert Laughlin**
Trebor's Vintage Watches
Montreal, Canada
www.vintagewatch.ca

**www.militarywatchbuyer.com**

**www.littlecogs.com**
J.E. Allnutt & Son Limited
West Street
Midhurst
West Sussex GU29 9NQ
Great Britain